the Staffordshire Bull Terrier

A guide to selection, care, nutrition, upbringing, training, health, breeding, sports and play.

Contents

Foreword

The book you are holding right now is by no means a complete book about the Staffordshire Bull Terrier. If we had collected all the information about the breed, its history and development, feeding, training, health, and whatever else there is to know, this book would have consisted of at least three hundred pages.

What we have done, however, is to bring together all the basic information that you as a (future) owner of a Staffordshire Bull Terrier need to know in order to handle your pet responsibly. Unfortunately, there are still people who buy a pet without thinking through what they are about to get into.

This book generally deals with the history of the breed, the breed standard and the advantages and disadvantages of buying a Staffordshire Bull Terrier. It also contains essential information about feeding your dog and about the very first steps in training it. Reproduction, day-to-day care, and health and illnesses are also topics.

After having read this book, you can make a carefully considered decision to buy a Staffordshire Bull Terrier and to keep it as a pet in a responsible manner. We advise you, however, not to rely on this book only. A well-reared and trained dog is more than just a dog. Invest therefore in a puppy training course or an obedience course. There are also plenty of excellent books that deal with certain aspects for which we do not have the space in this small book.

About Pets

A Publication of About Pets.

About Pets
co-publisher United Kingdom
Kingdom Books
PO9 5TL, England

ISBN 1852791977
First printing: December 2004
Second printing: May 2005

Original title: *de Staffordshire bull terrier*

About Pets bv,
Warffum, the Netherlands
www.aboutpets.info

Photos:
Rob Dekker, Isabelle Francoise, Kingdom
Books, Fam. Vandermeijden, Rene Verheul,
J. Klijn, I. Steijns,

Printed in China

In general

In past centuries, dogs with heavy heads, short muzzles and strong jaws used to be bred. Such dogs were praised for the same physical and mental characteristics that can be found in the Staffordshire Bull Terrier today.

Origins

The bulldog type originated from Molossers. These dogs were quite similar to today's Great Dane. Ever since prehistoric times, the Molossers were used as war dogs and, at the same time, to guard the storage rooms. These big dogs with their heavy heads, short snouts and strong jaws were known particularly for their fearlessness and their biting power. They were used on the battlefields to jump at the throats of horses and thus cause the enemy to fall.

When, due to changes in warfare techniques, these dogs became superfluous on the battlefields, their new role was to entertain the aristocracy by fighting against bears, bulls and wolves in the arena. The Celts had also bred a similar dog, the Mastiff.
Bull fights became increasingly popular in Great Britain. In this sport, the dog was used to fight against a bull. These dogs became known under the name of 'bulldog' or 'bull baiter', words originating from 'bull baiting', the original name of this sport.

When the English aristocracy lost its interest in bull baiting, it became a favourite pastime with the common people. The big dogs were, however, very expensive to keep and also difficult to house in a worker's home. People thus started to breed smaller, more mobile dogs. The bulls, which now had a clear advantage, were tied up in fights from now on.

At around 1830, dog fights gained popularity in England. The bulldogs of the time, with their short snouts and undershot jaws, were ideally built to grip the bull at its nose and to hold on for as long as necessary. This fighting technique was not as popular in dog fights (it was not spectacular enough). The search was on for dogs with longer muzzles, which grabbed their opponents again and again. Their teeth had to be bigger and their jaws had to close correctly to ensure a good bite. Shorter legs were also an advantage, as a dog with a low-lying centre of gravity is less easily knocked over. These dogs were called 'bulldog terriers'. The winner of a dog fight was the dog that refused to 'surrender'. The winning dog was thus not necessarily the best fighter. Even today, the most valued characteristics of the Staffordshire Bull Terrier are its fearlessness and its determination.

All animal fighting was prohibited later in the nineteenth century. The Staffordshire Bull Terrier thus had to survive almost a century as just a pet. The breeding focussed on preserving the breed-specific characteristics, whereby the breed was made more sociable so that it was more suited to its duties as a pet.

The English breed association was founded in Cradley Heath, Staffordshire, in 1935. This is how the dog got the name Staffordshire Bull Terrier.

Breed standard

A standard has been developed for all breeds recognised by the F.C.I. (Fédération Cynologique Internationale). The F.C.I. is the umbrella organisation of the Western European dog world. The officially approved breed associations of the member countries provide translations of the breed standard. This standard provides a guideline for breeders and judges. It is something of an ideal that dogs of each breed must strive to match. With some breeds, dogs are already being bred that match the ideal. Other breeds have a long way to go. There is a list of defects for each breed. These can be serious defects that disqualify the dog, in which case it will be excluded from breeding. Permitted defects are not serious, but do cost points in a show.

The UK Kennel Club Breed Standard for the Staffordshire Bull Terrier according to F.C.I. standard no. 76/23.06.88

General Appearance
Smooth-coated, well balanced, of great strength for its size. Muscular, active and agile.

Characteristics
Traditionally of indomitable courage and tenacity. Highly intelligent and affectionate especially with children.

Temperament
Bold, fearless and totally reliable.

Head and Skull
Short, deep though with broad skull. Very pronounced cheek muscles, distinct stop, short foreface, nose black.

Eyes
Dark preferred but may bear some relation to coat colour. Round, of medium size, and set to look straight ahead. Eye rims dark.

Ears
Rose or half pricked, not large or heavy. Full, drop or pricked ears highly undesirable.

Mouth
Lips tight and clean. Jaws strong, teeth large, with a perfect, regular and complete scissor bite, i.e. upper teeth closely overlapping lower teeth and set square to the jaws.

Neck
Muscular, rather short, clean in outline gradually widening towards shoulders.

Forequarters
Legs straight and well boned, set rather wide apart, showing no weakness at the pasterns, from which point feet turn out a little.

Shoulders well laid back with no looseness at elbow.

Body
Close-coupled, with level topline, wide front, deep brisket, well sprung ribs; muscular and well defined.

Hindquarters
Well muscled, hocks well let down with stifles well bent. Legs parallel when viewed from behind.

Feet
Well padded, strong and of medium size. Nails black in solid coloured dogs.

Tail
Medium length, low-set, tapering to a point and carried rather low. Should not curl much and may be likened to an old-fashioned pump handle.

Gait/Movement
Free, powerful and agile with economy of effort. Legs moving parallel when viewed from front or rear. Discernible drive from hindlegs.

Coat
Smooth, short and close. Colour red, fawn, white, black or blue, or any one of these colours with white. Any shade of brindle or any shade of brindle with white. Black and tan or liver colour highly undesirable.

Size
Desirable height at withers 36-41 cm (14 to 16 in), these heights being related to the weights. Weight: dogs: 13-17 kg (28-38 lb); bitches 11-15.4 kg (24-34 lb).

Faults
Any departure from the foregoing points should be considered a fault and the seriousness with which the fault should be regarded should be in exact proportion to its degree and its effect upon the health and welfare of the dog.

Note
Male animals should have two apparently normal testicles fully descended into the scrotum.

Reproduced with courtesy of the Kennel Club of Great Britain, September 2000

Buying your Staffordshire Bull Terrier

Once you have made that properly considered decision to buy a dog, you have various options. Do you want a puppy, an adult dog, or even an older dog? Would you rather have a bitch or a dog?

When choosing a Stafford, it is advisable to buy a pedigree dog. Of course, the question also arises as to where to get your dog; from a private person, a reliable breeder, or from an animal shelter? It is important for you and the animal that you sort out all theses things in advance, as you want to make sure that you get a dog that suits your circumstances. With a puppy, you choose a playful, energetic housemate that finds it easy to adapt to its new environment. If you prefer things a bit quieter, an older dog is a good choice. Contact the breed association about the possibilities of buying an adult dog.

Advantages and disadvantages

The Staffordshire Bull Terrier has been bred as a companion dog for many generations. It is therefore a friendly dog, oriented towards human company. The Stafford is very sociable and not at all shy. It will not wait for visitors to caress it, and will happily introduce itself. It is a dog of medium size and thus fits into almost any home quite well. The Stafford's coat is smooth and short and needs little care. The Staffordshire Bull Terrier is a sporty dog, which really enjoys going for walks or running next to the bike, and it possesses great stamina (when trained).

One of the disadvantages of the Staffordshire Bull Terrier is that it is a bad guard dog. If you are looking for a dog to protect house and hearth, you need to look at other breeds. Most Staffords also dislike water. If you are a fan of water sports, you might be better off choosing a gundog breed. Another very important point to bear in mind is that a Stafford will never miss a fight. It will not attack of its own accord, but should your Stafford get involved in a fight, there can quite easily be some serious casualties. Take this into consideration when thinking about buying a Staffordshire Bull Terrier. In many European countries, Staffordshire Bull Terriers are classed as dangerous dogs and are thus subject to certain laws and restrictions. This does not apply to the UK, however. Here they are actually one of the most commonly found breeds.

Male or female?

Whether you choose a male or a female puppy, or an adult dog or bitch, is an entirely personal decision. A male typically needs more leadership because he tends to be more dominant by nature. He will try to play boss over other dogs and, if he gets the chance, over people too. In the wild, the most dominant dog (or wolf) is always the leader of the pack. In many cases this is a male. A bitch is usually much more focussed on her master, as she sees him as the pack leader.

A puppy test is good for defining what kind of character a young dog will develop. During a test one usually sees that a dog is more dominant than a bitch. You can often quickly recognise the bossy, the adventurous and the cautious characters. So visit the litter a couple of times early on. Try to pick a puppy that suits your own personality. Explain to the breeder what type of dog you are looking for and what your plans are with the animal. Are you looking for a puppy with which you will be able to go to shows later, or would you prefer to do dog sports? Ask the breeder for advice, as he knows his puppies best. A dominant dog, for instance, needs a strong hand. It will often try to see how far it can go. You must regularly make it clear who's the boss, and that it must obey all the members of the family.

Puppy ...

When bitches are sexually mature, they will go into season. On average, a bitch is in season twice a year for about two to three weeks. This is the fertile

period when she can mate. Particularly in the second half of her season, she will want to go looking for a dog to mate with. A dog will show more masculine traits once he is sexually mature. He will make sure other dogs know what territory is his by urinating as often as possible in as many places as he can. He will also be difficult to restrain if there's a bitch in season nearby. As far as normal care is concerned, there is little difference between a dog and a bitch.

Puppy or adult?

After you've decided on a male or a female, the next question comes up. Should it be a puppy or an adult dog? Your household circumstances usually play a major role here. Of course, it's great having a sweet little puppy in the house, but bringing up a young dog takes a lot of time. In its first year it learns more than during the rest of its life. This is the period when the foundations are laid for elementary matters, such as house-training, obedience and social behaviour.

... or adult?

You must reckon with the fact that your puppy will keep you busy for a couple of hours a day, certainly in the first few months. You won't need so much time with a grown dog. It has already been brought up, but this doesn't mean it doesn't need correcting from time to time.

A puppy will no doubt leave a trail of destruction in its wake for the first few months. With a little bad luck, this will cost you some rolls of wallpaper, some good shoes and a few socks. In the worst case you'll be left with some chewed furniture. Some puppies even manage to tear curtains from their rails. With good upbringing this 'vandalism' will quickly disappear, but you won't have to worry about this if you get an older dog. However small a Staffordshire Bull Terrier puppy might be, it will manage to dismantle anything it can reach. It is therefore advisable to buy an indoor kennel for your puppy.

The greatest advantage of buying a puppy, of course, is that you can bring it up your own way. And the upbringing a dog gets (or doesn't get) is a major influence on its whole character. Finally, financial aspects may play a role in your decision. A puppy is generally (much) more expensive than an adult dog, not only in purchase price but also in 'maintenance'. A puppy needs to go to the vet's more often for the necessary vaccinations and check-ups.

Overall, bringing up a puppy requires a good deal of energy, time and money, but you have its upbringing in your own hands. An adult dog costs less money and time, but its character has already been formed. You should also try to find out about the background of an adult dog. Its previous owner may have formed its character in somewhat less positive ways.

Two dogs?

Having two or more dogs in the house is not just nice for us, but also for the animals themselves. Dogs get a lot of pleasure from company of their own kind. After all, they are pack animals. Although Staffordshire Bull Terriers are very focused on their master and family, they still enjoy more company and being with other dogs.

Staffordshire Bull Terriers can be kept together quite easily. If you're sure that you want two young dogs, it's best not to buy them at the same time. Bringing a dog up and establishing the bond between dog and master takes time, and you need to give a lot of attention to your dog in this phase. Having two puppies in the house means you have to divide your attention between them. Apart from that, there's a danger that they will focus on one another rather than on their master. Make sure that the age difference between the two dogs is approximately two years. This is because the Stafford matures quite late mentally (when it is approximately two years).

It is absolutely not a good idea to buy two male Staffordshire Bull Terriers. Two dogs might get along quite well for some time, but if they do start a fight at one point, they will probably never get along again afterwards.

Bitches can be kept together quite easily, but you do need to be aware of their character. Never put two dominant bitches together, as you can almost guarantee that this couple will start a fight. Bitches do fight once in a while, but they can normally be left together again after a short time. In practice, there are a lot of breeders who keep several bitches together.

An even better combination is a dog and a bitch, as dogs are quite happy to endure bitches with an attitude. You do need to bear in mind, of course, that the bitch will come on heat, and that you need to keep the bitch and the dog separated during this time if you want to avoid having puppies.

It is advisable to keep two Staffords apart at night, and also not to leave them in a room together without supervision. Do not take any risks, and stick to having only one dog if you cannot keep them apart.

A dog and children

Dogs and children are a great combination. They can play together and get great pleasure out of each other's company. Moreover children need to learn how to handle living beings; they develop respect and a sense of responsibility by caring for a dog (or another pet).

However sweet a dog is, children must understand that it is an animal and not a toy. A dog isn't comfortable when it's being messed around with. It can become frightened, nervous and even aggressive as a result. So make it clear what a dog likes and what it doesn't. Look for ways the child can play with the dog, perhaps a game of hide-and-seek where the child hides and the dog has to find it. Even a simple tennis ball can provide enormous pleasure. Children must learn to leave a dog in peace when it doesn't want to play any more. The dog must therefore have its own place where it's not disturbed. Let your children help with your dog's care as much as possible. A strong bond will be the result.

The arrival of a baby also means changes in the life of a dog. Before the birth you can help get the dog acquainted with the new situation. Let it sniff at the new things in the house and it will quickly accept them. When the baby has arrived, involve the dog in day-by-day events as much as possible, but make sure it gets plenty of attention too.

Never leave a dog alone with young children! Crawling infants sometimes make unexpected movements, which can easily frighten a dog. Infants are also hugely curious, and may try to find out whether the tail is really fastened to the dog, or whether its eyes come out, just like they do with their cuddly toys. But a dog is a dog and it will defend itself when it feels threatened.

Where to buy

There are various ways of acquiring a dog. The decision for a puppy or an adult dog will also determine to a great extent where you buy your dog.

If it is to be a puppy, you need to find a reliable breeder with a litter. If you choose a popular breed such as the Staffordshire Bull Terrier, you will have plenty of choice. This also means, however, that you will come across dogs that have only been bred for profit's sake. You can see how many puppies are for sale by looking in the classified section of your local newspaper every Saturday. Some of these dogs have pedigrees, but many don't. In so-called 'puppy farms', breeders also often do not look out for breed-specific illnesses and in-breeding. The puppies are taken away from the mother as quickly as possible and are thus insufficiently socialised. Never buy a puppy which is too young and of which you did not get to see the mother and/or the papers.

What to watch out for

Buying a puppy is no simple matter. You must pay attention to the following:

- Never buy a puppy on impulse, even if it is love at first sight. A dog is a living being that will need a lot of care and attention over a period of twelve to fourteen years. It is not a toy that you can put away when you're done with it.
- When re-homing a dog, do not make a decision over night. Ask to take the dog on trial for a few weeks to see if you really get along.
- Take a good look at the mother. Is she calm, nervous, aggressive, well cared for or neglected? The behaviour and condition of the mother is not only a sign of the quality of the breeder, but also of the puppy you're about to buy.
- Avoid buying a puppy whose mother has been kept in a kennel only. A young dog needs as many different impressions as possible during its first few months, including living in a family. It gets used to people and possibly other pets this way. Kennel dogs miss these experiences and are inadequately socialised as a result.
- Always ask to see the parents' papers (vaccination certificates, pedigrees, official health examination reports).
- Never buy a puppy younger than eight weeks.
- Put all agreements with the breeder in writing. A model agreement is available from the breed association.

Luckily, there are plenty of bona-fide breeders of Staffordshire Bull Terriers in the UK. Try to visit several breeders before buying a puppy. Also find out if the breeder is willing to help you after you have bought the puppy and to help you look for solutions if problems should arise.

Finally, you must realise that a pedigree is nothing more or less than a proof of descent. The Kennel Club also issues pedigrees to the young of parents that suffer from congenital conditions, or that have never been checked for them. A pedigree says nothing about the health of the parent dogs.

If you would rather buy an adult dog, you can contact the breed association. They sometimes help with re-homing adult dogs that can no longer be kept by their owners due to circumstances (such as impulse buying, moving home, divorce or work-related matters).

Travelling with your Staffordshire Bull Terrier

There are a few things to think about before travelling with your dog. While one dog may enjoy travelling, another may hate it.

While you might enjoy going on holidays to far-away places, it is questionable whether your Stafford does, too.

That very first trip

The first trip of a puppy's life is also the most nerve-wrecking. This is the trip from the breeder's to its new home. If possible, pick up your puppy in the morning. It then has the whole day to get used to its new situation. Ask the breeder not to feed the puppy that day. The young animal will be overwhelmed by all kinds of new experiences. Firstly, it's away from its mother; it's in a small room (the car) with all its different smells, noises and strange people. So there's a big chance that the puppy will be carsick this first time, with the annoying consequence that it will remember travelling in the car as an unpleasant experience.

It's thus important to make this first trip as pleasant as possible. When picking up your puppy, always take someone with you who can sit in the back seat with the puppy on his or her lap and talk to it calmly. If it's too warm for the puppy, a place on the floor at the feet of your companion is ideal. The pup will lie there relatively quietly and may even take a nap. Ask the breeder for a cloth or something else that has been lying in the nest and thus has a familiar scent. The puppy can lie on this in the car, and it will also help if it feels lonely during the first nights at home.

If the trip home is a long one, then stop for a break (once in a while). Let your puppy roam and sniff around (on the lead!), offer it a little drink of water and, if necessary, let it do its business. Do take care to lay an old towel in the car. It can happen that the puppy, in its nervousness, may urinate or be sick. It's also good advice to give a puppy positive experiences with car journeys as soon as possible. Make short trips to nice places where you can walk and play with it. It can be a real nuisance if your dog doesn't like travelling in a car. There will always be times when you need to take your dog somewhere in the car, for example to the vet's or to visit family and friends.

Taking your Staffordshire Bull Terrier on holidays

When making holiday plans, you also need to think about what you're going to do with your dog during that time. Are you taking it with you, putting it into kennels or leaving it with friends? In any event there are a number of things you need to do in good time.

If you want to take your dog with you, you need to be sure in advance that it will be welcome at your holiday destination, and what the rules there are. As mentioned earlier, some countries class Staffords as dangerous dogs and thus subject them to special rules. Therefore check if any such rules apply at your travel destination if you intend to go abroad. If travelling to foreign countries, your dog will need certain vaccinations and a health certificate, which normally need to be done four weeks before departure. You must also be sure that you've made all the arrangements necessary to bring your dog back home to the UK, without it needing to go into quarantine under the rabies regulations. Your vet can give you the most recent information. If your trip is to southern Europe, ask for a treatment against ticks (you can read more about this in the 'Parasites' chapter).

Be careful if you're planning to go to southern Europe. There are certain mosquito species that can transmit the larvae of the heartworm. Dogs become infected by mosquito bites. The larvae can grow into worms more than 20 cm (8 in) long. These parasites

remain in the heart or in the pulmonary artery. Grown worms can cause serious health problems. When fighting heartworms, remains of the worms can cause problems in the blood vessels. Ask your vet about a safe treatment against heartworms if your travel destination is in southern Europe.

Although you might like the idea of taking your dog on holidays with you, you need to ask yourself honestly if your pet enjoys it as much. Staffords won't enjoy travelling to a hot country, as they don't cope well with heat. Travelling in the car for days is also not normally their preference. Some dogs badly suffer from carsickness. There are good treatments available, but you need to ask yourself whether you are really doing your dog a favour with them.

If you do decide to take your dog with you, make regular stops at safe places during your journey, as your dog needs to have a good run once in a while. Take plenty of fresh drinking water with you, as well as enough of the food your dog is used to. Don't leave your dog in the car standing in the sun. It can quickly be overcome by the heat, which can have fatal consequences. If you really cannot avoid it, park the car in the shade as far as possible and open a window a bit for fresh air. Even if you have taken these precautions: Never stay away long!

Always bear in mind that Staffords generally do not cope well with heat. Due to their coat, they can easily become overheated. Adapt the amount of exercise to the weather. Don't go for hour-long walks during the day, don't let your dog run beside the bike and don't let it chase after balls or sticks. On hot summer days, try to go for walks early in the morning or later in the evening. During the day, limit walks to a small stroll round the block. Also don't take your Staffordshire Bull Terrier to the beach on hot days. Although there is water available, there is still a big risk of your dog suffering a heatstroke.

If you are travelling by plane or ship, you need to inform yourself well in advance whether your dog is allowed to go with you and what rules apply. Allow plenty of time for your preparations, so that you can find an alternative if necessary.

Maybe you decide not to take your dog with you, and you then need to find somewhere for it to stay. Arrangements for a place in kennels need to be made well in advance. Certain vaccinations will be required, which need to be given a minimum of one month before the stay.

If your dog can't be accommodated in the homes of relatives or friends, it might be possible to have an acquaintance stay in your house. This also needs to be arranged well in advance, as it may be difficult to find someone who can do this. Always ensure that your dog can be traced should it run away or get lost while on holiday. A little tube with your address, or a tag with home and holiday addresses, can avoid a lot of problems.

Moving home

Dogs generally become more attached to humans than to the house they live in. Moving home is usually not a problem for them. But it can be useful to let your dog get to know its new home and the area around it before moving.

If you can, leave your Stafford somewhere else (with relatives, friends, or in kennels) on the day of the move. The chance of it running away or getting lost is then practically non-existent. Once you have completed your move, you can pick your dog up and let it quietly get familiar with its new environment. Give it its own place in the house at once and it will quickly adapt. At the beginning, always walk your dog on a lead, because an animal can get lost in new surroundings too. Always take a different route so that it gets to know the neighbourhood well.

Don't forget to get your new address and phone number engraved on your dog's tag. Send a change of address notice to the institution that has any chip data. Dogs must sometimes be registered in a new community (just as people), and you will be sent a bill for a dog licence. In many communities, you get part of your licence fee back if you move within the year you paid for.

Feeding your Staffordshire Bull Terrier

A dog is actually more of an omnivore than a carnivore. In the wild it would eat its prey complete with skin and fur, including the bones, stomach, and the innards with their semi-digested vegetable material.

In this way the dog supplements its meat menu with the vitamins and minerals it needs. This is also the basis for feeding a domestic dog.

Ready-made foods

It's not easy for a layman to put together a complete menu for a dog, including all the necessary proteins, fats, vitamins and minerals in just the right proportions and quantities. Meat alone is certainly not a complete meal for a dog, as it contains too little calcium. A continuous calcium deficiency will lead to bone defects, and particularly for a fast-growing puppy this can cause serious skeletal deformities. If you put its food together yourself, you can easily give your dog too much in terms of vitamins and minerals, which can also be bad for your dog's health.

You can avoid these problems by giving your Stafford ready-made food of a good brand. These products are well balanced and contain everything your dog needs. Supplements, such as vitamin preparations, are superfluous. The amount of food your dog needs depends on its weight and activity level. You can find guidelines on the packaging.

Split the food into two meals per day if possible, and ensure that there's always a bowl of fresh drinking water next to its food. Give your Stafford the time to digest its food and don't let it outdoors straight after a meal. A dog should also never play on a full stomach. This can cause stomach torsion (the stomach turning over), which can be fatal for your dog.

Because the nutritional needs of a Stafford depend, among other things, on its age and way of life, there are many different types of dog food available. There are "light" foods for less active dogs, "energy" foods for working dogs and gundogs and "senior" foods for older dogs.

Canned foods, mixers and dry foods

Ready-made foods, which are available at pet shops or in the supermarket, can roughly be split into canned food, mixer and dry food. Whichever form you choose, ensure that it's a complete food with all the necessary nutrients. You can see this on the packaging.

Most dogs love canned food. Although the better brands are composed well, they do have one disadvantage: they are soft. A dog fed only on canned food will sooner or later have problems with its teeth (plaque, paradontosis). Besides canned food, give your Stafford dry foods or dog chews at certain times.

Mixer is a food consisting of chunks, dried vegetables and grains. Almost all the moisture has been extracted. The advantages of mixer are that it is light and keeps well. You add a certain amount of warm water and the meal is ready. A disadvantage is that it must definitely not be fed without water. Without the extra fluid, mixer will absorb the fluids present in the stomach, which can cause serious problems. Should your dog manage to get at the bag and enjoy its contents, you must immediately give it plenty to drink.

Dry foods also have had moisture extracted, but not as much as mixer. The advantage of dry foods is that they are hard, forcing the dog to use its jaws. During chewing tartar is removed and the gums are massaged.

Dog chew products

Naturally, once in a while you want to spoil your dog with something extra. Don't give it pieces of cheese or sausage as these contain too much salt and fat. There are various products available at pet shops that a dog will find delicious and which are also healthy, especially for its teeth. You'll find a large range of varying quality in the pet shop.

The butcher's left-overs

The bones of slaughtered animals have traditionally been given to the dog, and dogs are crazy about them, but they are not without risks. Pork and poultry bones are too weak for a Staffordshire Bull Terrier's strong jaws. They can splinter and cause serious injury to the intestines. Beef bones are more suitable, but they must first be cooked to kill off dangerous bacteria. Pet shops carry a range of smoked, cooked and dried abattoir residue, such as pigs' ears, bull penis, tripe sticks, oxtails, gullet, dried muscle meat and hoof chews.

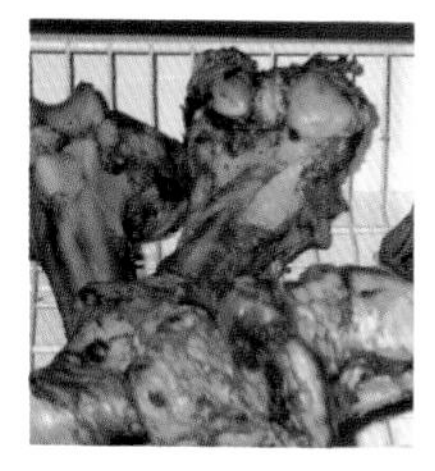

Smoked bones

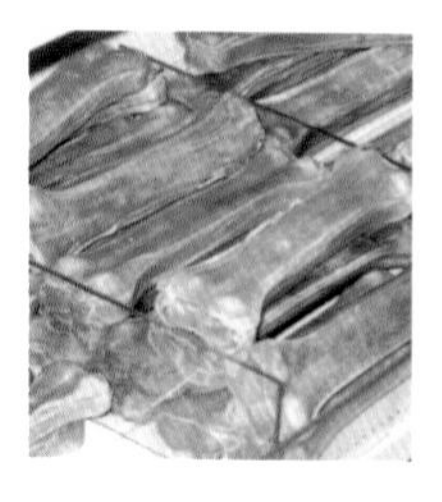

Cowhide chews

Fresh meat

If you do want to give your dog fresh meat occasionally, never give it raw, but always boiled or roasted. Raw (or not fully cooked) pork or chicken can contain life-threatening bacteria. Chicken can be contaminated by the notorious salmonella bacteria, while pork can carry the Aujeszky virus. This disease is incurable and will quickly lead to your pet's death.

Cowhide and buffalo hide chews

Dog chews are usually made of buffalo hide or cowhide. The hide is pressed or knotted into chews. Your dog can enjoy chews in the form of little shoes, twisted sticks, lollies, balls and various other shapes. Nice to look at and a nice change. Never buy chews that are too small, as they can easily go down the wrong way if the dog becomes greedy. Throw away small left-over bits of dog chews.

Munchie sticks

Munchie sticks are green, yellow, red or brown coloured sticks of various thicknesses. They consist of ground buffalo hide with a number of often undefined additives. Dogs usually love them because these sticks have been dipped in the blood of slaughtered animals. The composition and quality of these between-meal treats is not always clear. Some are fine, but there have also been sticks found that contained high levels of cardboard and even paint residues. Choose a product whose ingredients are clearly labelled.

Overweight?

Recent investigations have shown that many dogs are overweight. A dog usually becomes too fat because of over-feeding and lack of exercise. Use of medicines or a disease is rarely the cause.

Dogs that become too fat are often given too much food or too many treats between meals. Gluttony or boredom can also be a cause, and a dog often puts on weight following castration or sterilisation. Due to changes in hormone levels it becomes less active and consumes less energy. Finally, simply too little exercise alone can lead to a dog becoming overweight.

You can use the following rule of thumb to check whether your dog is overweight: you should be able to feel its ribs, but not see them. If you can't feel its ribs then your dog is much too fat. Overweight dogs live a passive life; they play and run too little and tire quickly. They also suffer from all kinds of medical problems (problems in joints and heart conditions). They usually die younger too.

So it's important to make sure that your dog doesn't become too fat. Always follow the guidelines on food packaging. Adapt them if your dog is less active or gets lots of snacks. Try to ensure that your dog gets plenty of exercise by playing and running with it as much as you can. If your dog starts to show signs of putting on weight, you can switch to a low-calorie food. If it's really too fat and reducing its food quantity doesn't help, then a special diet is the only solution.

Munchie sticks

Caring for your Staffordshire Bull Terrier

Good (daily) care is extremely important for your dog. A well cared-for dog is less likely to become ill after all.

Caring for your dog is not only necessary but also a pleasure, as master and dog give each other all their attention for a moment. It is also a good opportunity for playing and cuddling.

The coat

Good coat care involves regularly brushing or combing the coat and checking for parasites. How often a dog needs to be brushed or combed depends on the length of the coat. The Stafford has a short, smooth coat and therefore does not need to be brushed very often. It is, however, advisable to brush it on a regular basis, especially during moulting, so that all loose hair is removed from the coat. Be aware that your Stafford will lose hair throughout the year and that you will find it all over the house. It is thus preferable to brush your dog outdoors, as you will then have less trouble with dog hair flying all over the house.

Always use the right tools when caring for your dog's coat. Combs must not be too sharp. Choose a brush made of rubber or natural hair. Always brush from head to tail, following the direction the hair lays in. If you get your Stafford used to having its coat cared for from a young age, it will quickly learn to enjoy its grooming sessions. Regularly check your dog for fleas and ticks (also see chapter 'Parasites').

Only bathe your Staffordshire Bull Terrier when it is absolutely necessary, and always use a special dog shampoo when doing so. Make sure that no shampoo can get into your dog's ears and eyes, and always rinse the suds out well. Only let your dog out when it is completely dry, as dogs can catch colds too! Your vet can prescribe certain medicinal shampoos for different skin conditions. Always follow the instructions. Good flea control is very important to prevent skin and coat disorders.

You need to fight fleas not only on the dog itself, but also in its environment. Coat problems can also be the result of allergies to certain feed components. In this case, the vet can prescribe a hypoallergenic diet.

Teeth

Your Stafford needs to be able to eat properly to stay in good condition. It thus needs healthy teeth. Therefore check your dog's teeth regularly. If you think that all is not well, contact your vet. Regular feeds of hard dry food help to keep your dog's teeth clean and healthy. There are special dog chews that help to prevent build-up of tartar and to keep the breath fresh.

The best way to keep your dog's teeth healthy is by brushing them regularly. You can use a special toothbrush for dogs for this, but a piece of gauze wrapped round a finger will also do the job. If you get your dog used to having its teeth cleaned at a young age, you won't have any problems later. You can also get an older dog used to having its teeth cared for. With a dog treat as a reward, it certainly won't mind.

Nails

On a Stafford with healthy round feet that regularly walks on hard surfaces the nails will grind themselves down to the right length. It is not necessary to clip them in this case. It won't do any harm, however, to check the length of its nails at certain times, especially on dogs that don't go out on the streets a lot or that only walk on soft ground. Also remember to check the fifth nail on the inside of the front paws. This nail does not wear off, as it does not touch the ground. With the help of a piece of paper, you can easily see if your dog's nails are too long. If you can push the paper between the ground and the nail of the (standing) dog, the nail has the right length.

Nails that are too long can bother a dog. It can injure itself when scratching. They thus need to be cut back. You can do this with special scissors, which you can buy in the pet shop. Be careful not to cut the nail too far back, as you might cut into the quick. This can bleed profusely. If you feel unsure about cutting your dog's nails, let the vet or a grooming parlour do this necessary task.

Eyes

You need to clean your dog's eyes every day, as 'sleepies' and bits of dried tear fluid can collect in the corners of the eyes. You can easily remove these by wiping downwards with your thumb. If you do not like doing this, you can use a bit of toilet paper or a tissue.

Cleaning your dog's eyes only takes a few seconds a day, so don't miss it! If the sleepies become yellow and slimy, it is usually a sign of a serious irritation or an infection. Eye drops (available from your vet's) usually solve this problem quite quickly. Conditions of the third eyelid need to be corrected surgically.

Ears

The ears are often forgotten when caring for dogs, but they must be checked at least once a week. If your dog's ears are very dirty or have too much wax, you must clean them. This should preferably be done with a clean cotton cloth, which is moistened with some warm water or babyoil. It is inadvisable to use cotton wool due to the fluff it can leave behind. Never enter the ear canal with an object. If your Stafford is constantly shaking its head or scratching at its ears, you need to check them for ear mites. Your vet can prescribe a treatment to kill off the mites.

Bringing up your Staffordshir Bull Terrier

It is very important that your Stafford is well brought up and that it listens to you. This will make it not only more pleasant for you, but also for your environment.

A puppy can learn what it may and may not do in a playful manner. Rewarding and consistency are very important aids when bringing up your dog. If you always reward it for good behaviour with your voice, a pat or a treat, it will quickly learn to obey. A puppy course can help you along the way.

The life expectancy of a Staffordshire Bull Terrier is twelve to fourteen years. They mature quite late, but they also stay young, both physically and mentally, quite long. A good upbringing is thus very important for your puppy.
The Staffordshire Bull Terrier is a very sporty dog, which enjoys walking and running next to the bike, and it has great stamina.

(Dis)obedience

A dog that won't obey you is not just a problem for you, but also for your surroundings. It's therefore important to avoid unwanted behaviour. In fact, this is what training your dog is all about, so get started early. 'Start 'em young!' should be your motto.

An untrained dog is not just a nuisance, but can also cause dangerous situations by running into the road, chasing joggers or jumping at people. A dog must be trained out of this undesirable behaviour as quickly as possible. The longer you let it go on, the more difficult it will become to correct. The best thing to do is to attend a special obedience course. This won't only help to correct the dog's behaviour, but its owner also learns how to handle undesirable behaviour at home. A dog must not only obey its master during training, but at home too.

Always be consistent when training good behaviour and correcting annoying behaviour. This means your dog may always behave in a certain way, or must never behave that way. Think about whether you will find a puppy's behaviour, such as snapping at hands and jumping at people, acceptable with an adult dog. Always reward your dog for good behaviour and never punish it after the event for any wrongdoing. If your dog finally comes after you've been calling it a long time, then reward it. If you're angry because you had to wait so long, it may feel it's actually being punished for coming. It will probably not obey at all next time for fear of punishment.

Try to take no notice of undesirable behaviour, as your dog will perceive your reaction (even a negative one) as a reward for this behaviour. If you need to

correct your dog, then do it immediately. Use your voice or grip it by the scruff of its neck and push it to the ground. This is the way a bitch calls her pups to order. Rewards for good behaviour are, by far, preferable to punishment; they always achieve a better result.

When bringing up your Staffordshire Bull Terrier, bear in mind that, despite their appearance, they are very good-natured, friendly dogs. They cannot cope with too much pressure. If you put your dog under too much pressure when bringing it up, it will result in undesirable behaviour. It is much better for your Staffordshire Bull Terrier if you bring it up in a playful manner. Your dog is very sensitive to your voice and thus not difficult to teach. Staffordshire Bull Terriers are also very intelligent and enjoy working for their master.

House-training

The very first training (and one of the most important) that a dog needs is house-training. The basis for good house-training is keeping a close eye on your puppy. If you pay attention, you will notice that it will sniff around a long time and turn around a certain spot before doing its business there. Pick it up gently and place it outdoors, always at the same place. Reward it abundantly if it does its business there.

Another good moment for house-training is after eating or sleeping. A puppy often needs to do its business at these times. Let it relieve itself before playing with it, otherwise it will forget to do so and you'll not reach your goal. For the first few days, take your puppy out for a walk just after it's eaten or woken up. It will quickly understand your intention, especially if it's rewarded with a dog biscuit for a successful attempt.

Of course, it's not always possible to go out after every snack or snooze. Lay newspapers at different spots in the house. Whenever the pup needs to do its business, place it on a newspaper. After some time it will start to look for a place itself. Then start to reduce the number of newspapers. Finally, there will be just one newspaper left, at the front or back door. The puppy will learn to go to the door if it needs to relieve itself. Then you put it on the lead and go out with it. You can eventually remove the last newspaper. Your puppy is now house-trained.

One thing that certainly won't work is punishing an accident after the event. A dog whose nose is rubbed in its urine or its droppings won't understand that at all. It will only get frightened of you. Here too, rewarding works much better than punishment. An indoor kennel or cage can be a good tool to help in house-training. A puppy won't foul its own nest, so a kennel can be a good solution for the night, or during periods in the day when you can't watch it. But an indoor kennel must not become a prison where your dog is locked up day and night.

First exercises

The basic commands for an obedient dog are those for sit, lie down, come and stay. You can teach a pup to sit by holding a piece of dog biscuit above its nose and then slowly moving it backwards. The puppy's head will also move backwards until its hind legs slowly go down. At that moment you call 'Sit!'. After a few attempts, it will quickly remember this nice game. Use the 'Sit!' command before you give your dog its food, put it on the lead, or before it's allowed to cross the street.

Teaching the command to lie down is similar. Instead of moving the piece of dog biscuit backwards, move it down vertically until your hand reaches the ground and then forwards. The dog will also move its forepaws forwards and lie down on its own. At that moment call 'Lie down!' or 'Lay!'. This command is useful when you want your Stafford to be quiet.

Two people are needed for the 'Come!' command. One holds the dog back while the other runs away. After about fifteen metres (50 ft), he stops and enthusiastically calls 'Come!'. The other person now lets the dog go, and it should obey the command at once. Again you reward it abundantly. The 'Come!' command is useful in many situations and good for safety too.

A dog learns to stay from the sitting or lying position. While it's sitting or lying down, you call the command 'Stay!' and then step back one step. If the dog moves

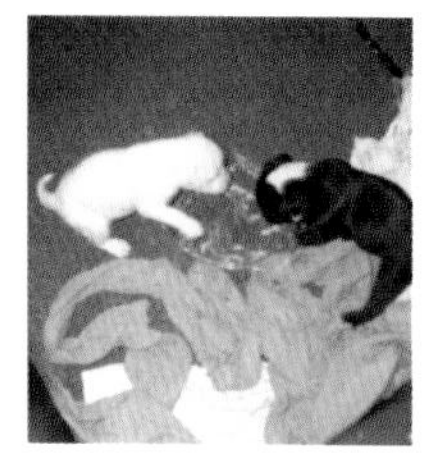

with you, quietly put it back in position, without displaying anger. If you do react angrily, you're actually punishing it for coming to you, and you'll only confuse your dog. It can't understand that coming is rewarded one time, and punished another. Once the dog stays nicely, reward it abundantly. Practise this exercise while increasing the distances between your dog and yourself (at first no more than one metre/ 3 ft). The 'Stay!' command is useful when getting out of the car.

Obedience courses

Obedience courses to help you bring up your dog are available throughout the UK. These courses do not just teach owner and dog a lot, but are also fun. Make sure that you ask about the method of training in advance. Look for a dog school where the emphasis is on rewarding good behaviour. If the dogs are rewarded too little, your Stafford will soon lose its interest and fun in training. Teaching good behaviour has to be done in a playful manner.

With a puppy, you can begin with a puppy training course. This is designed to provide the basic training. A puppy that has attended such a course has learned about all kinds of things that will confront it in later life: other dogs, humans, traffic and more. The puppy will also learn obedience and to follow a number of basic commands. Apart from all that, attention will be given to important subjects such as grooming, being alone, travelling in a car, and doing its business in the right places.

The next step after a puppy course is a course for young dogs. This course repeats the basic exercises and ensures that the growing dog doesn't get into bad habits. After this, the dog can move on to an obedience course for fully grown dogs.

For more information on where to find courses in your area, contact your local kennel club. You can get its address from the Kennel Club of Great Britain in London. In some areas, the RSPCA organises obedience classes and your local branch may be able to give you information.

Play and toys

There are various ways to play with your Stafford. You can romp and run with it, but also play a number of games, such as retrieving, tug-of-war, hide-and-seek and catch. A tennis ball is ideal for retrieving, and you can play tug-of-war with an old sock or a special tugging rope. Start with tug-of-war only when your dog is a year old. A puppy must first get its second teeth and then they need several months to strengthen. There's a real chance of your dog's teeth becoming deformed if it starts playing tug-of-war too soon. You can use almost anything for a game of hide-and-seek. Frisbees are ideal for catching games. Never use too small a ball for games, as it can easily get lodged into the dog's throat.

Play is extremely important. Not only does it strengthen the bond between dog and master, but it's also healthy for both. Make sure that you're always the one that ends the game. Only stop when the dog has brought back the ball or frisbee, and make sure that you always win the last tug-of-war. This confirms your dominant position in the hierarchy. Use these toys only during play, so that the dog doesn't forget their significance.

When choosing a special dog toy, remember that dogs are hardly careful with them. So always buy toys of good quality, which a Stafford can't easily destroy.

Be also very careful with sticks and twigs. The latter, particularly, can easily splinter. A splinter of wood in your dog's throat or intestines can cause awful problems. Throwing sticks or twigs can also be dangerous. If they stick into the ground, a dog can easily run into them with its mouth open.

If you want to do more than just playing the odd game with your dog, you can do lots of different types of dog sports. If you are looking for a challenge, have a look at different activities such as flyball, dogfrisbee, agility and obedience certificates (see chapter 'Sports and shows').

Aggression

Staffordshire Bull Terriers are normally never aggressive towards humans. They were used as fighting dogs in the past, but they were never trained to attack people. This is why they are also no good as farm dogs or guard dogs. It can, however, happen that your Stafford is less friendly towards other animals or people. It is therefore good to have some background information about aggression in dogs. There are two different main types of aggressive behaviour in dogs: The anxious-aggressive dog and the dominant-aggressive dog.

An anxious-aggressive dog can be recognised by its pulled-back ears and its lowly held tail. It will have pulled in its lips, baring all teeth including the molars. This dog is aggressive because it's very frightened and feels cornered. It would prefer to run away, but if it can't then it will bite to defend itself. It will grab its victim anywhere it can. The attack is usually brief and as soon as the dog can see a way to escape it's gone. In a confrontation with other dogs it will normally turn out as the loser. It can become even more aggressive once it's realised that people or other animals are afraid of it. You can't change this behaviour just like that. You first have to try to understand what the dog is afraid of. Getting professional help is a good idea here, as the wrong approach can easily make the problem worse.

The dominant-aggressive dog's body language is very different. Its ears are pricked and its tail is raised and stiff. This dog will go only for its victim's arms, legs or throat. It is self-assured and highly placed in the dog hierarchy. Its attack is a display of power rather than a consequence of fear. This dog needs to know who's the boss. You must bring it up rigorously and with a strong hand. An obedience course can help.

A dog may also show aggression when in pain. This is a natural defensive reaction. In this case try

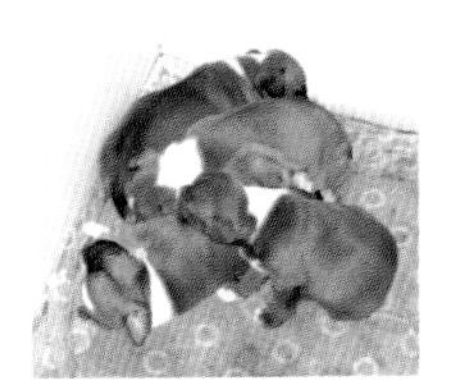

to resolve the dog's fear as far as possible. Reward it for letting you get to the painful spot. Be careful, because a frightened dog in pain may also bite its master! Muzzling it can help prevent problems if you have to do something that may be painful. Never punish a dog for this type of aggression!

Fear

If your dog behaves in a frightened manner, the reason can usually be found in the first few weeks of its life. A lack of new experiences in this very important so-called 'socialisation phase' has a big influence on the adult dog's behaviour. If a dog does not get to see humans, other dogs or other animals during this phase, it will be afraid of them later. This is common with dogs that have grown up in a barn or kennel with basically no human contact. As mentioned earlier, fear can lead to aggression. It is thus very important that your dog gets as many new experiences as possible during its first few weeks. Take it into town in the car or on the bus, walk down a busy street with it and let it have lots contact with people, other dogs and other animals/ pets.

It's a huge task to turn an anxious, poorly socialised dog into a real pet. It will probably take an enormous amount of attention, love, patience and energy to get such an animal used to everything around it. Reward it often and give it plenty of time to adapt and, over time, it will learn to trust you and become less anxious. Try not to force anything, because that will always have the reverse effect. Here too, an obedience course can help a lot.

A dog can be especially afraid of strangers. Have visitors give it something tasty as a treat when they arrive. Put a can of dog biscuits by the door, so that your visitors can spoil your dog when they come in the door. Once again, don't try to force anything. If the dog is still frightened, it is best to leave it in peace.

Dogs are often frightened in certain situations; well-known examples are thunderstorms and fireworks. In these cases try to ignore your dog's anxious behaviour. If you react to its whimpering and whining, it's the same as rewarding it. If you ignore its fear completely, your dog will quickly learn that nothing is wrong. You can speed up this 'learning process' by rewarding its positive behaviour.

Rewarding

Rewarding forms the basis for bringing up a dog. Rewarding good behaviour works far better than punishing bad behaviour and rewarding is also much more fun. Over time the opinions on how to bring up dogs have gradually changed. In the past, a sharp pull on the lead was considered the appropriate way to correct bad behaviour. Today, experts view rewards as a positive incentive to get dogs to do what we expect of them.

There are many ways of rewarding your Stafford. The usual ways are a pat or a friendly word, even without a tasty treat to go with it. When bringing up a puppy, a tasty treat at the right moment will do wonders, though. Make sure that you always have something tasty in your pocket to reward it for good behaviour.

Another form of reward is play. Dogs love to play. Whenever your dog notices that you have a ball in your pocket, it won't go far from your side. As soon as you've finished playing, put the ball away. This way your dog will always do its best in exchange for a game. Despite the emphasis you put on rewarding good behaviour, a dog can sometimes be a nuisance or disobedient. You must correct such behaviour immediately. Always be consistent: once 'no' must always be 'no'.

Barking

Dogs that bark too much and too often are a nuisance for their surroundings. A dog-owner may tolerate barking up to a point, but neighbours are often annoyed by the unnecessary noise. Luckily, Staffordshire Bull Terriers do not bark excessively by nature. It might still happen, however, that your puppy imitates and adopts the yapping of other dogs in the area. Don't encourage your puppy to bark and yelp in that case. Of course, it should be able to announce its presence, but if it goes on barking it must be called to order with a strict 'Quiet!'. If the puppy does not obey, you can hold its muzzle closed with your hand for a moment.

A dog will sometimes bark for long periods when left alone. It feels threatened and tries to get someone's attention by barking. If a dog has been (sub)consciously rewarded for barking, it can carry on with this behaviour for some time. There are special training programmes for this problem, where a dog learns that being alone is nothing to be afraid of, and that its master will always return.

This is how you can practise with your dog: Leave the room and come back in at once. Reward your dog if it stays quiet. Gradually increase the length of your absences and keep rewarding it as long as it remains quiet. Never punish your dog if it does bark or yelp. It will never understand punishment afterwards, and this will only make the problem worse. Never go back into the room as long as your dog displays the unwanted behaviour, as it will view this as a reward.

You might want to make your dog feel more comfortable by switching the radio on for company during your absence. It will eventually learn that you always come back and the barking will reduce. If you don't get the required result, attend an obedience course with your dog.

Reproductior

Dogs, and thus also Staffordshire Bull Terriers, follow their instincts, and reproduction is one of nature's most important processes. This is of benefit to people who enjoy breeding dogs.

After the mating the dogs are 'stuck'

Those who simply want a 'cosy companion' however, will miss the regular adventures with females on heat and unrestrainable males like a hole in the head. But knowing a little about the reproduction of dogs will help you to understand why they behave the way they do, and what measures you need to take when this happens.

Liability

There is much more connected to breeding dogs than simply 1+1= many. If you're planning to breed with your Staffordshire Bull Terrier, be on your guard. The whole affair can quite easily turn into a financial disaster, because, under the law, a breeder is liable for the 'quality' of his puppies. It is also advisable to ensure that both animals have full papers. Be therefore meticulous in your search for a mating partner for your dog.

The breed association places high demands on animals used for breeding. They need to be checked for possible (hereditary) abnormalities. By applying to these rules, a breeder shows that he cares. If you breed a litter and sell the puppies without these tests having been made, you can be held liable by the new owners for any possible costs resulting from any hereditary abnormality! And these (vet's) bills can be very expensive! It is therefore advisable to contact a breed association if you're thinking about breeding a litter.

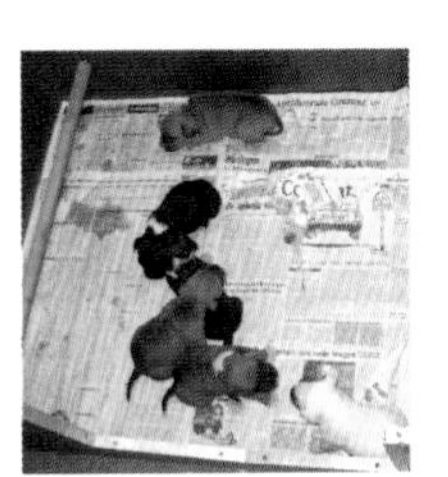

The female in season

Staffordshire bitches become sexually mature at the age of six to twelve months. With this breed, there are a lot of bitches that have their first season when they are six to seven months old. This is quite young for dogs. A normal season lasts two to three weeks. During this time, the bitch loses drops of blood and is very appealing to males. The bitch is fertile during the second half of her season, and she will then accept dogs to mate. The best time for mating is between the ninth and thirteenth day of her season.
A female's first season is often shorter and less severe than those that follow. If you want to breed with your bitch, you must allow the first (and sometimes the second) season to pass. Most bitches go into season twice per year.

If you do plan to breed with your Staffordshire Bull Terrier bitch in the future, then sterilisation is not an option to prevent unwanted offspring. A temporary solution is a contraceptive injection, although this is controversial because of possible side effects such as womb infections.

Phantom pregnancy

A phantom pregnancy is a not uncommon occurrence with dogs. The female behaves as if she has a litter. She takes all kinds of things to her basket and treats them like puppies. Her milk teats swell up and sometimes milk is actually produced. The female will sometimes behave aggressively towards people or other animals, as if she is defending her young.

Phantom pregnancies usually begin two months after a season and can last a number of weeks. If it happens to a bitch once, it will often re-occur after every season. If she suffers under it a lot, sterilisation is the best solution, because constantly re-occuring phantom pregnancies increase the risk of womb or teat conditions.

In the short term a hormone treatment is worth trying, perhaps also homeopathic medicines. Camphor spirit can give relief when teats are heavily swollen, but rubbing the teats with ice or a cold cloth (moisten and freeze) can also help relieve the pain. Feed the female less than usual, and make sure that she gets enough distraction and extra exercise.

Preparing to breed

If you do plan to breed a litter of puppies, you must first wait for your female to be physically and mentally fully grown before you have her covered. In any event you must wait until her second

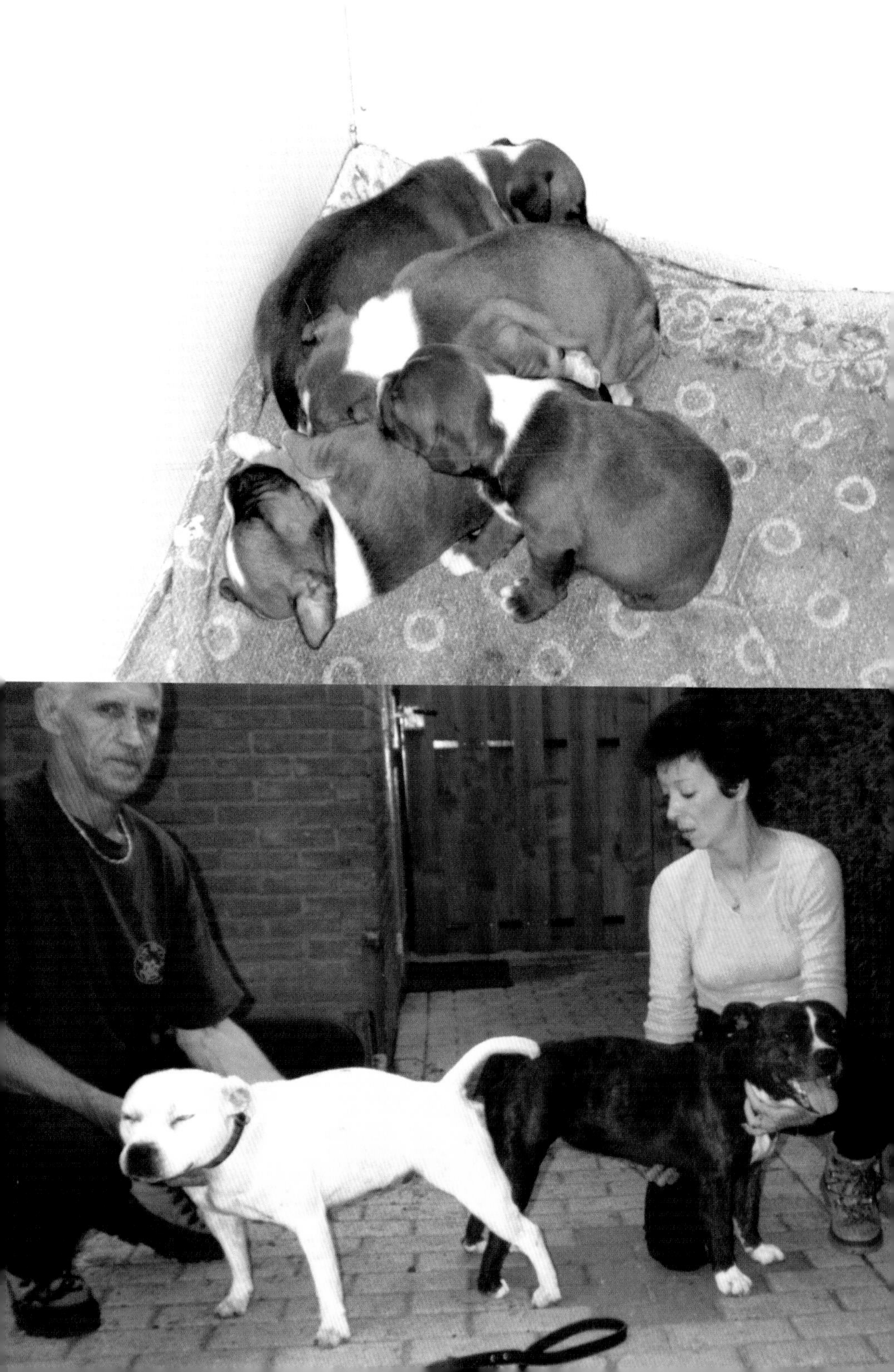

season. To mate a bitch, you need a male, preferably with a pedigree. In those countries where Staffords are classed as dangerous dogs breeding animals are required to have full F.C.I. pedigrees. You could simply let your bitch out on the street and she would quickly return home pregnant. If you want to be serious about breeding, you should therefore keep a close eye on your bitch in season and never let her run free.

Think especially about the following: Accompanying a bitch through pregnancy, birth and the first eight to twelve weeks afterwards is a time-consuming affair. Never breed with Staffordshire Bull Terriers that have congenital defects, and this also applies to dogs with full papers. The same goes for hyperactive, nervous and shy dogs.

Contact one of the clubs on page 60 or 61 for more information on breeding and breeding regulations.

Pregnancy

It's often difficult to tell at first if a bitch is pregnant. Only after about four weeks can you feel the pups in her belly. She will now slowly become fatter and her behaviour will usually change. Her teats will swell during the last few weeks of pregnancy. The average pregnancy lasts 63 days and costs the bitch a lot of energy. In the beginning she is fed her normal amount of food, but her nutritional needs increase in jumps during the second half of the pregnancy. Give her approximately fifteen percent more food each week from the fifth week on. The mother-to-be needs extra energy and proteins during this phase of her pregnancy. During the last weeks you can give her a concentrated food that is rich in energy, such as dry puppy food. Divide this into several small portions per day, as the bitch can no longer deal with large portions of food. Towards the end of the pregnancy, her energy needs can easily be one-and-a-half times more than usual.
After about seven weeks the mother will start to demonstrate nesting behaviour and to look for a place to give birth to her young. This might be her own basket or a special birthing box. This must be ready at least a week before the birth to give the mother-to-be time to get used to it. The basket or box should preferably be in a quiet place.

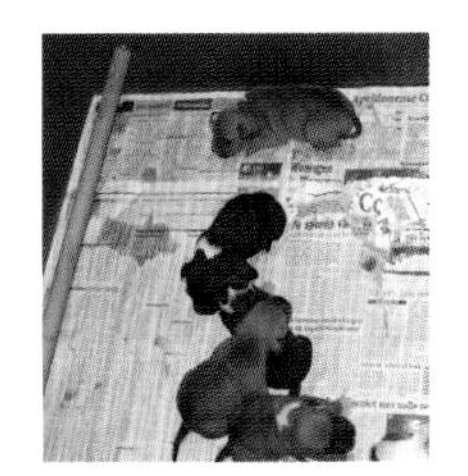

Birth

On average, three to nine puppies are born in a litter. The birth normally passes without problems. If you are in any doubt, you need to contact your vet immediately, of course!

Birth by cesarian

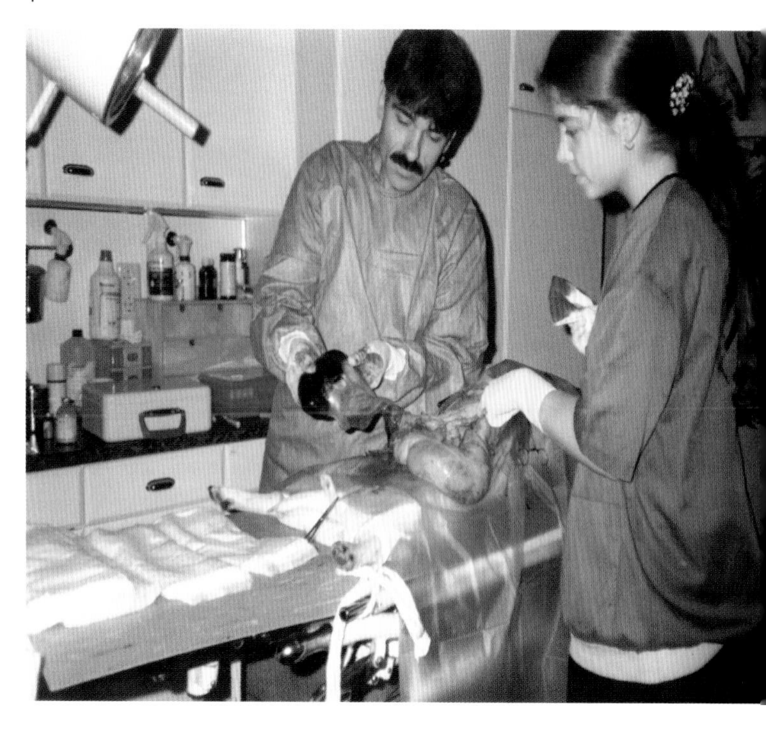

Suckling and weaning

After giving birth, the mother starts to produce milk. The suckling period is very demanding. During the first three to four weeks the pups rely entirely on their mother's milk. During this time she needs extra food and fluids. This can be up to three to four times the normal amount. If she's producing too little milk, you can give both the mother and her young special puppy milk.

Here too, divide the high quantity of food the mother needs into several smaller portions. Again, choose a concentrated high-energy food and give her plenty of fresh drinking water. Do not give the bitch cow's milk, as this can cause diarrhoea.

You can give the puppies some supplemental solid food when they are three to four weeks old. There are special puppy foods available that follow on well from the mother's milk and that can easily be eaten with the puppies' milk teeth.

Ideally, the puppies are fully weaned at an age of six to seven weeks, i.e. they no longer drink their mother's milk. The mother's

milk production gradually stops and her food needs also drop. Within a few weeks after weaning, the mother should be back to getting the same amount of food as before the pregnancy.

Castration and sterilisation

As soon as you are sure that your bitch should never bear a (new) litter, a vasectomy or sterilisation is the best solution. During sterilisation (in fact this is normal castration) the ovaries and often the uterus are removed surgically. The bitch no longer goes into season and can no longer become pregnant. The best age for a sterilisation is about eighteen months, when the bitch is more or less fully grown.

A male dog is usually only castrated for medical reasons or to correct undesirable sexual behaviour. During a castration the testicles are removed, which is a simple procedure and usually without complications. There is no special age for castration but, where possible, wait until the dog is fully grown. Vasectomy is sufficient where it's only a case of making the dog infertile. In this case the dog keeps its sexual drive but can no longer reproduce.

Sports and shows

Staffordshire Bull Terriers love to be active. They enjoy doing things with their master. These dogs are also real allrounders.

If you regularly participate in activities with your Stafford, you will notice not only that the bond between both of you is becoming stronger, but also that your dog is a lot quieter in the house and a lot more obedient. Contact the breed association or dog schools in your area if you want more information on all the different sporting and showing opportunities.

Agility

Agility is a sport during which a dog has to master a certain course accompanied by its owner. The course consists of approximately twenty obstacles, which need to be mastered faultlessly in a certain order without faults and as quickly as possible. The owner may direct the dog through the course with voice commands and gestures. The task is to overcome the obstacles as quickly as possible and with as few faults as possible. Agility competitions are organised by a lot of local kennel clubs.

Dogfrisbee

This is a sport that originated in America. The dog is required to catch a frisbee, which can be thrown in different ways. A special flexible dogfrisbee is used, which does not damage the dog's teeth. There are two different classes. The 'freestyle' class is accompanied by music. The thrower has 120 seconds to show as many throwing techniques as possible, and the dog has to catch the frisbee as often as possible. The other class is called 'minidistance'. Here, the thrower has only 60 seconds to throw the frisbee as far as possible. The further the frisbee flies, the more points the thrower receives.

Flyball

Flyball is another form of dog sports. A flyball team consists of dog owners, their dogs, a coach and a person loading the balls into the apparatus. The number of participants can vary from five to eight dog/ owner combinations. First the dog has to jump over four small hurdles, and then it has to push down a plank on the flyball apparatus with its paw. This action 'launches' a ball, which the dog needs to catch. The dog has to jump over the hurdles again on its way back and carry the ball to its owner as quickly as possible. The combination with the fastest time wins here too.

Behaviour and obedience

You can choose from a wide variety of obedience training courses, starting with puppy courses. Staffords normally really enjoy this type of training: as they are very focused on their master, they will happily try to carry out the exercises as well as possible. After the basic obedience training courses, you can carry on training for obedience diplomas.

Dog shows

Visiting a dog show is a pleasant experience for both dog and master, and for some dog-lovers it has become an intensive hobby.

They visit countless shows every year. Others find it nice to visit an exemption show with their dog just once. It's worth making the effort to visit an exemption show where a judge's experienced eyes will inspect your Staffordshire Bull Terrier and assess it for build, paces, condition and behaviour. The judge's report will teach you your dog's weak and strong points. This can be very useful when choosing a mate for breeding, for example. You can also exchange experiences with other Stafford owners. Official dog shows are only open to dogs with pedigrees.

Ring training

If you've never been to an exemption show, you're probably tapping in the dark in terms of what will be expected of you and your dog. Many kennel clubs organise so-called ring training courses for dogs going to an exemption show for the first time. This training teaches you exactly what the judge will be looking for, and you can practise the correct techniques together with your dog.

Club matches

Almost all kennel clubs and breed associations organise club matches. You have to enter your dog in a certain class before the big day. These meetings are usually small and friendly and are often the first acquaintance dog and master make with a judge.

This is an overwhelming experience for your dog - a lot of its contemporaries and a strange man or woman who fiddles around with it and peers into its mouth. After a few times, your dog will know exactly what's expected of it and will happily go to the next club match.

Championship shows

Various championship shows take place during the course of the year, all of which offer different prizes. These shows are much more strictly organised than club matches. Here, too, your dog must be registered in a certain class in advance and it will then be listed in a catalogue. On the day itself, the dog is kept in a cage (indoor kennel) until its turn comes up. During the judging in the ring, it's important that you show your dog at its best. The judge will give an official verdict and write a report. When all the dogs from that class have been judged, the winner is selected. You can pick up your report, and possibly your prize, after the class has finished.

The winners of the various classes will then compete for the title of Best of Breed. A winner will be chosen from the dogs belonging to the same breed group. The various winners of the different breed groups will then compete for Best in Show.

It goes without saying that your dog has to be in top condition for a show. The judge will not be pleased if your dog's coat is dirty and its paws are covered in mud. Its nails must be clipped and the teeth free of tartar. The dog must also be free of any parasites or illnesses. A bitch must not be in season, and a dog should have both its testicles. Judges also don't like badly brought up, frightened or nervous dogs. If you want to know more about (exemption) shows, contact your local kennel club or the breed association.

Do not forget!

If you want to visit a show with your Staffordshire Bull Terrier, you need to be well prepared. You must certainly not forget the following:

For yourself:

- Registration card
- Food and drink
- Safety pin for the catalogue number
- Chair(s)

For your dog:

- Food and drink bowls and food
- Dog blanket and perhaps a cushion
- Show lead
- A brush
- Vaccination book and other papers for your dog

Parasites

All dogs are vulnerable to various sorts of parasites. Parasites are tiny creatures that live at the expense of another animal. They feed on blood, skin and other body substances. There are two main types.

Internal parasites live within their host animal's body (tapeworm and roundworm) and external parasites live on the animal's exterior, usually in its coat (fleas and ticks), but also in its ears (ear mite).

Fleas

Fleas feed on a dog's blood. They cause not only itching and skin problems, but can also carry infections such as tapeworm. In large numbers they can even cause anaemia and dogs can also become allergic to a flea's saliva, which can cause serious skin conditions.

So it's important that you treat your dog for fleas as effectively as possible. Do not just treat the animal itself, but also its surroundings. There are various medicines for treating your dog: drops for the neck and to put in its food, flea collars, long-life sprays and flea powders. There are various sprays in pet shops, which can be used to eradicate fleas in your dog's immediate surroundings. Choose a spray that kills both adult fleas and their larvae. If your dog goes in your car, you should spray that too.

Fleas can also affect other pets, so you should treat those too. When spraying a room, cover any aquarium or fishbowl present. If the spray reaches the water, it can be fatal for your fish! Your vet and pet shop have a wide range of flea treatments and can advise you further on the subject.

Ticks

Ticks are small, spider-like parasites. They feed on the blood of the animal or person they've settled on. A tick looks like a tiny, grey-coloured leather bag with eight feet. When it has sucked itself full, it is darker in colour and can easily be five to ten times its own size.

Dogs usually fall victim to ticks in bushes, woods or long grass. Ticks cause not only irritation by their blood-sucking, but can also carry a number of serious diseases. This applies especially to the Mediterranean countries, which can be infested with blood parasites. In our country these diseases are fortunately less common. But Lyme disease, which can also affect humans, has reached our shores. Your vet can prescribe a special treatment if you're planning to take your dog to southern Europe. It is important to fight ticks as effectively as possible. Check your dog regularly, especially when it's been running free in woods and bushes. It can also wear an anti-tick collar.

Removing a tick is simple using tick tweezers. Grip the tick with the tweezers, as close to the dog's skin as possible, and carefully pull it out. You can also grip the tick between your fingers and, with a turning movement, pull it carefully out. You must disinfect the spot where the tick was, using iodine to prevent infection. Never soak the tick in alcohol, ether or oil. In a shock reaction the tick may discharge the infected contents of its stomach into the dog's skin.

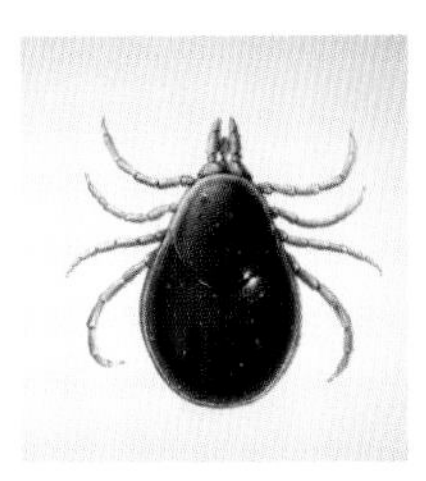

Tick

Worms

Dogs can suffer from various types of worm. The most common are tapeworm and roundworm. Tapeworm causes diarrhoea and poor condition. With a tapeworm infection you can sometimes find small pieces of the worm around the dog's anus or on its bed. In this case, the dog must be wormed immediately. You should also check your dog for fleas, as these can transmit the tapeworm infection.

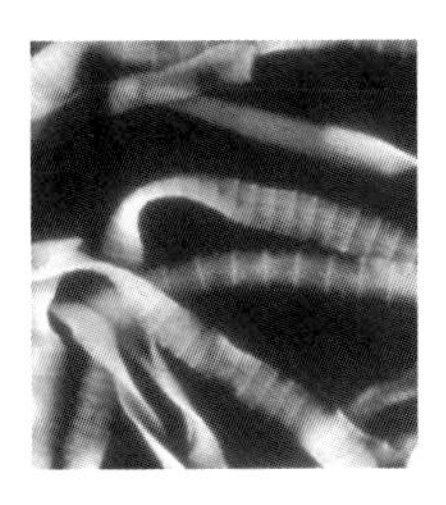

Tapeworm

Roundworm is another condition that reoccurs regularly. Puppies are often infected by their mother's milk. Roundworm causes problems (particularly in younger dogs), such as diarrhoea, loss of weight and stagnated growth. In serious cases the pup becomes thin, but with a swollen belly. It may vomit and you can then see the worms in its vomit. They are spaghetti-like tendrils. In its first year, a puppy regularly needs to be treated with a worm treatment. Adult dogs should be treated twice a year.

Roundworm

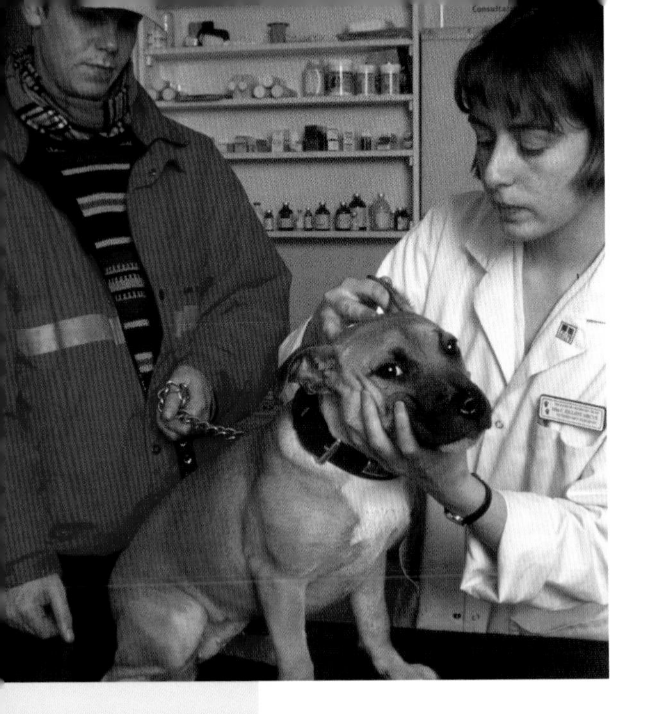

Your Staffordshire Bull Terrier's health

The Staffordshire Bull Terrier is a very healthy dog breed. No specific hereditary disorders are known of. Just as any other dog, however, your Stafford can become ill.

Anal gland disease

A dog that scoots over the ground with its bottom might be suffering from Anal Gland Disease (impacted anal glands). In this case you must empty the glands (or let the vet do it). You can feel the anal glands under the dog's tail, at the anus. If you think of a clock, these glands are positioned at around twenty to four. Your vet can teach you when and how to empty the anal glands (by squeezing them).

Corona

Corona is a virus disease that is accompanied by vomiting and diarrhoea. The symptoms are similar to those of a Parvo infection, but they are less severe. Apart from the symptoms mentioned under Parvo, Corona can also affect the mucous membranes. The symptoms for this are discharge from the eyes and nose. The disease is spread via excrements.

Rabies

This virus disease is fatal for humans and dogs alike. The virus is transmitted via saliva, and it enters the body via (small) wounds. Rabies spreads via the nerves all the way to the brain, which eventually causes the victim's death. After being bitten by an infected animal, it can take up to fifty days for the first symptoms to appear in the victim. The last phase of the illness is horrendous. At this point the virus has affected the brain, the dog is scared and crawls away into a corner, and its behaviour can turn into being wild and very aggressive. It will then destroy and attack anything in its surroundings. Luckily, Rabies does not exist in the UK (and quarantine laws are in place to keep it this way), but it can be found in continental Europe. If you plan to travel abroad with your dog, it needs to be vaccinated against Rabies. The disease is transmitted by saliva (bites) of foxes, badgers and other animals.

Canine Distemper

This illness, also known as Carré's Disease, is caused by a virus and is very infectious. The severity of the first symptoms, a runny nose and a little coughing, is often underestimated. Shortly after the first symptoms, fever, lack of appetite, vomiting and/or diarrhoea follow. Inflammation of the throat, pus-like discharge from nose and eyes, twitching and cramps follow. A young dog may become critically ill. The virus

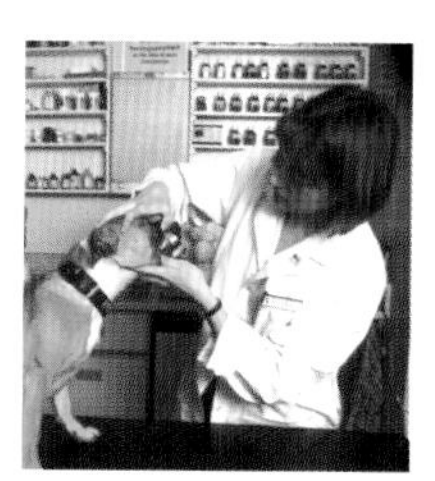

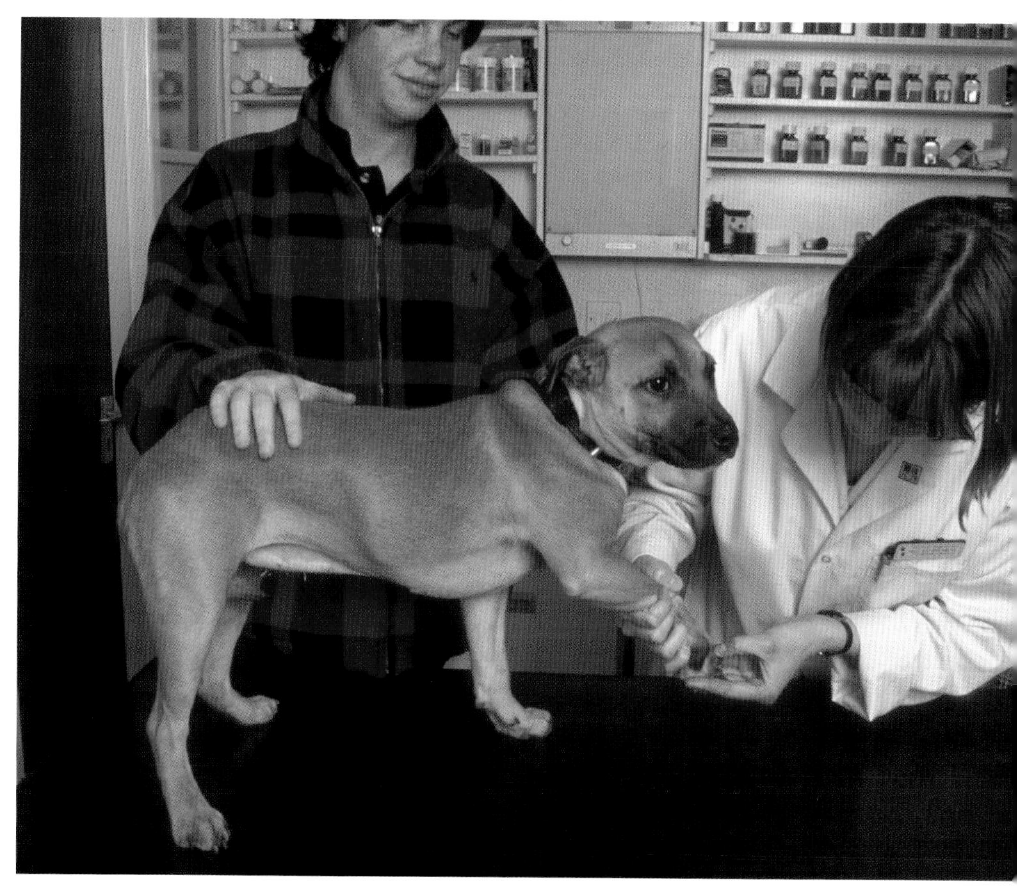

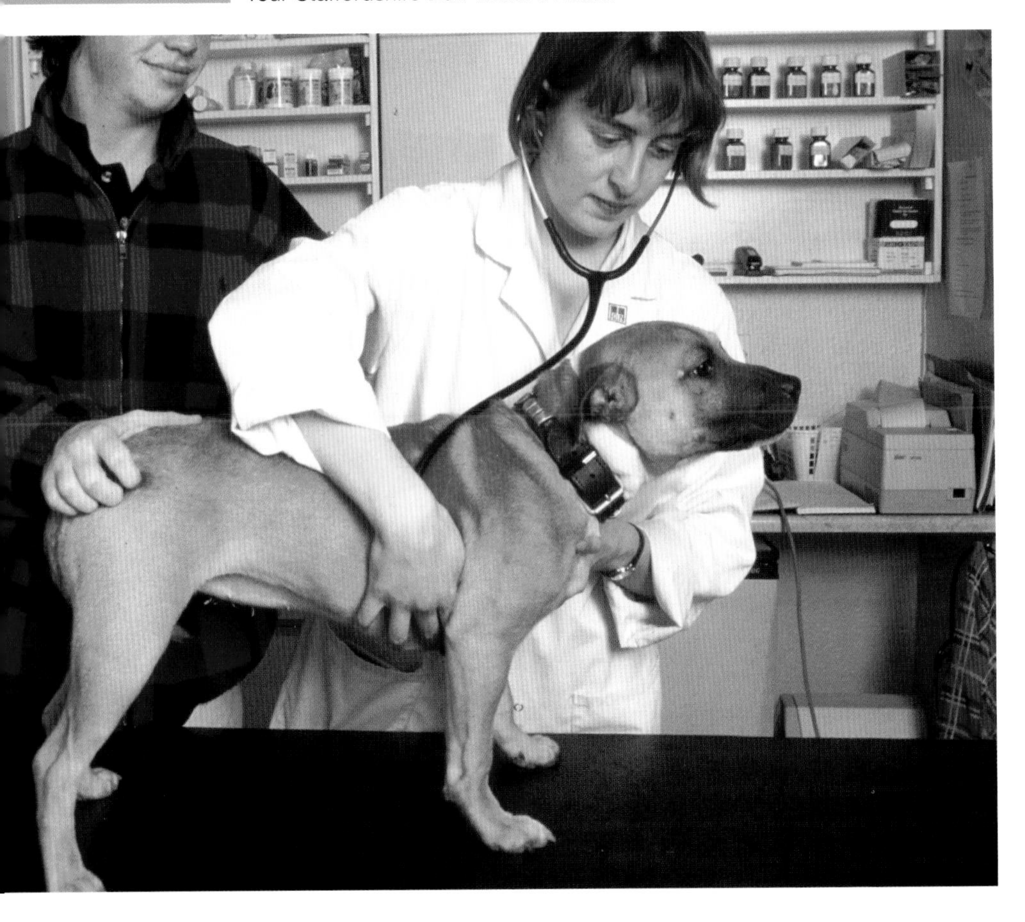

causes inflammations in the intestines, but also Meningitis. A lot of dogs do not survive this disease. Of the dogs that do survive, many are left with permanent nerve damage, or at least a 'tic'. The dog will often display a behavioural disorder that it did not have before the illness, e.g. it finds it difficult to orientate itself or gets lost quickly. Canine Distemper is spread via saliva, urine and excrements.

Kennel Cough

The Kennel Cough Syndrome is an illness that is caused by various microorganisms, including Parainfluenza virus, Bordetella virus and others. Infection usually occurs where a lot of dogs are together, for example in a (boarding) kennel, at a show or on dog training grounds. This ailment of the respiratory system presents itself with a harsh scratchy cough, which is sometimes combined with damage to the lungs. Most of the time, the dogs aren't too ill, but they still need to be treated by a vet. The mucous membranes can be eased with cough medicine (thyme syrup) and taking your dog on a short break with lots of fresh air can do wonders. If you are leaving your dog in boarding kennels, it is advisable (and often mandatory) to vaccinate it as a precaution against this stubborn cough four weeks before you leave. Transmission is via the breath.

Parvo

Parvo is a highly contagious disease that is caused by a virus. A dog infected by the Parvovirus will often die. The virus is spread via the excrement of an infected dog. When healthy dogs sniff at this excrement, they become infected straight away. The virus spreads to the intestines, where it causes serious inflammation. Within a very short time, the dog will suffer from bloody diarrhoea, might vomit blood, will become drowsy, have a temperature and become critically ill. It will usually refuse to eat and drink and can thus become dehydrated. Most dogs die of dehydration in combination with a severe loss of blood. Treatment therefore mainly consists of administering large amounts of fluids by infusion. Most dogs die within 48 hours after the first symptoms appear. In puppies, an infection can cause heart failure. Today, puppies are vaccinated against Parvo while still in the litter. Puppies that survive the illness might suddenly die later on in life due to Myocarditis, a heart condition that can be caused by Parvo.

Weil's Disease

Weil's Disease (Leptospirosis) is a disease caused by microorganisms. The biggest chance of infection is in the spring and autumn. The disease can be fatal in younger dogs. Humans can also be infected by dogs and rats. A dog swimming in or drinking from contaminated water might be infected by bacteria via the mucous membranes and possibly small skin wounds. The bacteria establish themselves in the liver and kidneys. The symptoms are: high fever, doziness and muscle pain. The dog also lacks any appetite, vomits and is very thirsty. It might also have nosebleed, dark urine and sometimes Yellow Fever. The disease is transmitted via the urine of infected dogs and rats.

Breed associations

Becoming a member of a breed club can be very useful for good advice and interesting activities. Contact the Kennel Club in case addresses or telephone numbers have changed.

Alyn & Deeside Staffordshire Bull Terrier Club
Sec. Mr A Moran
Tel No: 0161 320 6485

Downlands Staffordshire Bull Terrier Club
Sec. Mrs A Gatenby
Tel No: 01730 828402
www.downlands.org.uk

East Anglian Staffordshire Bull Terrier Club
Sec. Mrs L McFadyen
Tel No: 01992 427698
www.eastangliansbtclub.co.uk

East Midlands Staffordshire Bull Terrier Club
Sec. Mrs N Vann
Tel No: 01664 840570
www.emsbtc.co.uk

Merseyside Staffordshire Bull Terrier Club
Sec. Mr R Blackle.
Tel No:0151 287 6822
www.msbtc.co.uk

Morecambe Bay & Cumbria Staffordshire Bull Terrier Club
Sec. Mr G H Earle
Tel No: 01697 320217

North Eastern Staffordshire Bull Terrier Club
Sec. Miss J M E McLauchlan
Tel No: 01642 783948

North Of Scotland Staffordshire Bull Terrier Club
Sec. Ms J A Smith
Tel No: Not availble - for more information contact The Kennel Club

North West Staffordshire Bull Terrier Club
Sec. Miss S Houghton
Tel No: 01942 708161
www.northwestsbtclub.co.uk

Northern Counties Staffordshire Bull Terrier Club
Sec. Mrs C Lee
Tel No: 01423 863829

Northern Ireland Staffordshire Bull Terrier Club
Sec. Mr B Millen
Tel No: 02890 431580

Notts & Derby District Staffordshire Bull Terrier Club
Sec. Mrs.Jenny Smith
Tel No: 01332 781062

Potteries Staffordshire Bull Terrier Club
Sec.Mrs S A Reader.
Tel No: 01782 611514

Scottish Staffordshire Bull Terrier Club
Sec. Mr Fleming
Tel No: 0141 763 2349
www.ssbtc.co.uk

Southern Counties Staffordshire Bull Terrier Club
Sec. Mr Meneer
Tel No: For further information contact the Kennel Club
www.scsbts.freeserve.co.uk

Staffordshire Bull Terrier Club
Sec. Mr J Beaufoy
Tel No: 01299 403382
www.thesbtc.com

Staffordshire Bull Terrier Club Of South Wales
Sec. Mr J Holle
Tel No: 01792 542606
www.sbtcsw.co.uk

Western Staffordshire Bull Terrier Society
Sec. Mr Grimwood
Tel No: 01495 759254

The Kennel Club
1 Clarges Street
London, W1J 8AB UK
Tel: 0870 606 6750
Fax: 020 7518 1058
www.the-kennelclub.org.uk

Tips for the Staffordshire Bull Terrier

- Buy your Stafford puppy via the breed association and from a recognised breeder.
- If possible, visit several breeders before buying your puppy.
- Always ask to see the parent animals' pedigrees and declarations of health.
- Make a purchase contract before buying your puppy.
- Attend a puppy training course with your dog. It teaches both dog and master a lot.
- Its first journey is quite an adventure for a puppy. Make sure it's a nice one!
- Never buy a puppy whose mother you weren't able to see.
- Regularly feed your Stafford hard dry food and give it a dog chew. This will keep your dog's teeth healthy.
- Make sure that your dog doesn't become overweight. Not too much food and plenty of exercise are the golden rules.
- Never leave a dog alone with small children.
- Do not let your puppy run endlessly after a ball or stick.
- Do not only treat fleas, but also their larvae.
- Organise a holiday stay or a dog sitter for your Stafford well in advance.

The Staffordshire Bull Terrier

Country of origin:	Great Britain
Original tasks:	Dog and badger fights, rat control
Present task:	Pet
Character:	Enthusiastic, friendly, attached to humans
Colours:	Brindle, red, fawn, white, black or blue, or one of these colours with white
Weight:	Dogs: 12.7 – 17.3 kg (28 – 38 lb) Bitches: 10.9 – 15.4 kg (24 – 34 lb)
Shoulder height:	35.6 to 40.6 cm (14.2 – 16.2 in)
Life expectancy:	12 to 14 years

THE BLACK & WHI[illegible]

VILLAGE TRAIL

A WALKER'S GUIDE

DAVID GORVETT

an[illegible]

LES LU[illegible]

Scarthin Books, Cromford, 1991.

THE BLACK & WHITE VILLAGE TRAIL
A WALKERS GUIDE

THE COUNTRY CODE

Enjoy the countryside and respect its life and work
Guard against all risk of fire
Fasten all gates
Keep your dogs under close control
Keep to public paths across farmland
Use gates and stiles to cross fences, hedges and walls
Leave livestock, crops and machinery alone
Take your litter home
Help to keep all water clean
Protect wildlife, plants and trees
Take special care on country roads
Make no unnecessary noise

Published 1991

Phototypesetting, printing by Higham Press Ltd., Shirland, Derbyshire

ISBN 0 907758 47 9

CONTENTS

THE BLACK AND WHITE TRAIL

Herefordshire . . .
A county of villages

Herefordshire is still a county of villages, and nowhere more so than in the lands along the Welsh border between the market towns of Leominster and Kington. Here are some of the finest "Black and White" villages in England, each with a wealth of half-timbered houses and cottages to delight the eye and stir the curiosity. Every house differs from its neighbour, some with perfectly aligned frames, others leaning precariously into the street and all posing questions to the visitor. What memories of happiness and tragedy, war and peace are locked away in these ancient walls?

For, despite their present-day quietness, these small settlements have known violent times when their 'front-line' position in the struggles between the Welsh and the English brought whole armies into their tiny streets. It was not until the final calming of the Marches in the Fifteenth century that the villagers could turn back to their seasonal rounds in the fields and orchards. It was then that the traditional form of timber-framed buildings was able to develop and produce the distinctive style that sets these villages apart today.

Fortunate in the fertility of the dark-red soil and the abundance of rivers and streams the villages flourished both as self-contained communities and as tiny market towns. Apart from the bitter strife of the English Civil War, which disturbed even this placid county, rural life prevailed, dominated by the demands of the seasons, year in, year out. By an accident of geology Herefordshire had no coal or mineral ores to attract the mines and factories of the Industrial Revolution.

Even the mountain wall to the west, for so long the source of anxiety, became a protection as the new railways from the industrialised Midlands turned away from its massive obstructions, leaving the villages in half-forgotten transport backwaters.

So the pattern of fields, hedges, lanes and paths became frozen in time to provide the present-day walker with a wealth of opportunities to tread the ways that countless generations have done before. Past ways to work are now paths to pleasure, along which the discerning visitor will find much to delight the mind as well as to stretch the limbs! The authors hope that with their guidance the reader will come to share their enjoyment of a part of an older England that has miraculously survived and which merits everyone's care and concern for its future - both the landscape and all those who dwell therein.

THE 600-YEAR OLD CRUCK HOUSE, EARDISLEY

The Black and White Trail

The Black and White Trail was developed in 1987 by David Gorvett as a means of encouraging visitors to take a closer look at the beautiful countryside and villages between Leominster and Kington in the west of Herefordshire. As the name suggests the trail is characterised by the large number of timbered and half-timbered houses in the area some dating from mediaeval times, others from more recent periods.

Purists might frown at the use of the phrase 'Black and White' as in some respects this suggests that the buildings looked like this when first built. In fact, it was the Victorians who moved away from traditional wattle and daub to brick between the oak beams. It was also during the last century that it became popular to finish buildings in a black and white veneer. In earlier times the oak would not have been coated and the wattle and daub would have reflected the colour of the local clay rather than a whitewash lime.

The trail was written up mainly for those travelling by car as it is virtually impossible to get from village to village by bus in a couple of days. Nevertheless, it has always been possible to make the journey by bicycle and probably with far more pleasure once off the beaten track. The authors are currently investigating better routes for cyclists.

It seemed wholly appropriate, however, that the trail should become the province of the walker in two ways. Firstly, to walk between the villages and to see the landscape in the round seemed more sensible than to peer from a car window. Secondly, for those not wishing to walk such distances, we have added a number of local village walks. They are much shorter but still introduce the visitor to each locality thus allowing time to savour the views, breathe fresh air and to rest awhile over a pint or pot of tea. In this way we hope you gain more from the trail than a fleeting glance.

How To Use the Book

The Walks

The book comprises nine village walks varying in length from one to four miles and the 62 mile Black and White walking trail. For the most part the landscape is gently undulating farmland with very few climbs so the walking is reasonably easy going. Most of the rambles have not been written up in recent years so for the walker it presents new opportunities to explore a lovely part of the country. The views of the surrounding hill ranges from Dinmore to Merbach and the Black Mountains or to the Radnor Forest are superb. Equally, aspects of church spires and towers, of orchards and Georgian farmhouses, of timber framed houses and historic villages characterise the trail. Approaching these villages on foot offers time to reflect on the landscape and its people, there's an anticipation of stories to be told and refreshment on hand, emotions that belong to a traveller on foot rather than a visitor with little time to spare.

The entire Black and White walking route and the accompanying village walks have been checked during the autumn of 1990. Any problems incurred during this research period have been raised with Hereford and Worcester County Council and in some instances the relevant Parish Councils. Many paths have been obstructed in the past and thus it is not surprising that some have fallen into disuse. However, the mood is changing and our thanks go to those Parish Councillors and other people who have co-operated with the County Council to improve our access to the countryside in recent years. Many of these paths are as ancient as the communities themselves and their continued use allow access to a worked landscape rather than a country park created purely for leisure purposes. Let us hope that many more Herefordshire paths will be improved before the end of the century.

Time

All of the walks are suitable for the casual walker and families as well as the rambler seeking perhaps to cover more ground. Allow plenty of time, however, so that there are moments to pause, to admire the views and to take refreshment in the villages. If using local buses this becomes fundamentally important.

For those attempting the entire trail it is possible that the hardened long distance walker will walk it in two or three days but for most of us it will be a four day expedition. Accommodation is available in all of the villages on the route so use the Route Planner in Appendix 1 to check your likely destination each day. Information is available at Tourist Information offices.

What To Wear

Herefordshire is renowned for its mild weather but it is best to be prepared, particularly in winter, for the chance shower, a sudden drop in temperature or a chilling wind. A waterproof can easily be packed into a small knapsack. The most important thing is to keep your feet dry as paths and tracks can become really wet and muddy after rain especially if trodden by livestock. Always carry a light snack to replenish energy between villages on the longer sections of the trail.

Public Rights of Way

The walks in the book follow public rights of way mainly, which means that you are entitled to pass along the way without obstruction. However, sometimes you will come across a problem such as crop in a field where the path has not been reinstated or where a stile has been blocked with rubbish. You are entitled to clear a blockage to get by or make a reasonable detour if necessary. It is equally important to report the problem to the Rights of Way section, Hereford and Worcester County Council, County Hall, Spetchley Road, Worcester, WR5 2NP, so that others benefit afterwards from your information.

We sometimes forget, nevertheless, that it is a working countryside and that cows churn up tracks, trees are felled and bales or balls of hay get stacked in field corners. Such changes can make the instructions in the text seem inaccurate especially when a hedge has been grubbed to make a larger field. Please bear with the authors when it comes to changes on the landscape and by all means let us know so that we can let others know in revised editions, hopefully!

Maps

The route descriptions and maps in the text should be sufficient for the reader to negotiate the walks successfully but for those who like reading maps the walks can be followed using the Landranger Sheets 148 Presteigne and Hay-on-Wye, 149 Hereford and Leominster or better still the Pathfinder sheets;
Leominster 994
Kington 993
Hay-on-Wye 1016
Mortimers Cross and Tenbury Wells 972.

Refreshment and Accommodation

There are numerous places of refreshment along the route and these are indicated in the trail description. Accommodation is also readily available in the villages as well as in Leominster and Kington where there are several hotels as well as guest house and inn facilities.

The Tourist Information Centres should be able to provide you with the relevant and up to date information. Listed below are the three local offices:
Hereford, Town Hall Annexe, St. Owen St., Hereford, HR1 2PJ. Tel: (0432) 268430.
Kington, there's a tourist information open to personal callers near to the Town Clock.
Leominster, 6 School Lane, Leominster, HR6 8AA. Tel: (0568) 6460.

Public Transport

Hereford is the main railhead for the area with direct trains from London, Birmingham, Cardiff and Manchester. Leominster also enjoys a good level of service from Cardiff, Hereford and Manchester although trains commence late afternoon on Sundays.
Telephone enquiries: (0743) 64041 or (0452) 29501.

Buses serving the villages commence from either Hereford or Leominster. The main service is from Hereford (Country Bus Station -five minutes walk from the railway station) to Weobley and Kington serving Woonton and Lyonshall. Contact Sargeant Brothers, Mill St., Kington. Tel: (0544) 230481. Eardisley is also served with four to five buses per day from Hereford. Contact Yeomans Motors, (0432) 356201. The other villages are usually served by buses from Hereford and Leominster on market days only at school times.

Using these services it is possible for local residents and visitors to walk sections of the route without retracing steps or messing about with cars. For example, it is feasible to catch the bus from Hereford to Eardisley or Weobley and walk to Kington for the return journey home.

It simply requires a little advance planning but it does help to keep local buses going and keep parking problems down in the villages. Try it, as you will find it is easier than you think! Hereford and Worcester County Council produce summary timetable booklets for the Kington and Leominster areas. They are available by post from the County Engineer and Planning Officer, Hereford and Worcester County Council, County Hall, Spetchley Road, Worcester, WR5 2NP.

Herefordshire Cider and Perry

Any seasoned cider drinker will tell you that the market is now dominated by three major cider companies - H. P. Bulmer of Hereford, the Taunton Cider company and Showerings of Shepton Mallet, the latter two being based in Somerset. They must produce and sell ninety percent of the cider and perry consumed in this country. Furthermore, the cider we tend to see in our local supermarket or pub is mainly pasteurised, pressurised and lacking in taste in comparison to natural cider.

Natural or traditional ciders, made with few or no additives or colouring and sold without being pressurised are still on sale in the county. In fact, there has been something of a small scale revival of the art in recent years with an increase in the number of farms or cideries producing traditional cider in a commercial manner. Dunkertons Cider company at Luntley near Pembridge, only a mile or so away from the trail, is a fine example and their replanting of old varieties of cider apple and perry pear trees is to be admired. The beverages are splendid particularly the perry. Not far off the Black and White Trail is Great Oak Cider near Almeley, where cider is produced on the farm from the fruit of the old orchards near to the farmhouse and is on sale to the public at very reasonable prices.

These are two examples of a small number of suppliers looking to satisfy a growing market who seek the genuine thing. Be warned though, cider is a beverage to be handled with care. It is splendid with a meal or as a refreshing drink after a walk but don't imbibe too much as it is toe-curling stuff. Bulmers and Westons supply many of the public houses on route so if you are fortunate you will come across real cider from these companies but be sure to try the real thing rather than a fizzy imitation!

Location Map and Key

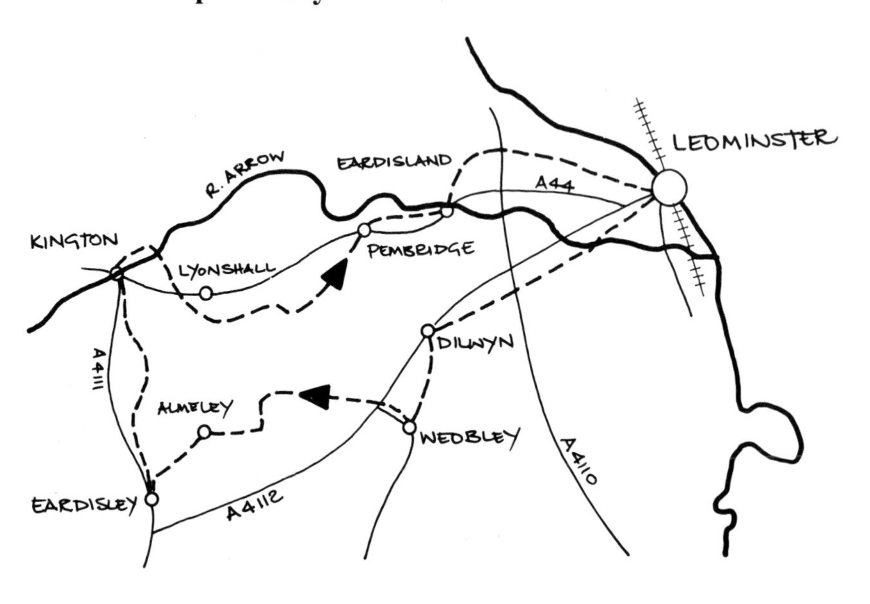

— — ▶ — —	route
– – – – –	path not on route
———	road
+++++——+++++	railway
++ ++ ++ ++	disused railway
∼∼ ∼∼	river/stream
+	church
▪▪	buildings
(tree symbols)	woodland
(star symbol)	historical site
③	number (3 etc.) corresponds with route description

Leominster

Outline Bus Station ~ Railway Station ~ T.I.C., School Lane ~ Town Trail.

Summary Fortunately, most of the ancient street pattern of the old market town of Leominster has survived the combined onslaught of traffic and the developers. A short walk following the excellent Town Trail illustrates this. Whilst time has not entirely stood still here it has paused enough for the observant visitor to be able to visualise the past, noting the mediaeval magnificence of the Priory, the prosperous years of the seventeenth and eighteenth centuries when timber framed buildings were at their finest, and the Georgian and Victorian houses and Assembly Rooms of the last century.

Situated almost midway between Hereford and Ludlow on the Marches rail link between Crewe and Cardiff, Leominster is the administrative centre of a large area of the border country. It still keeps some of its market activities but these have been changed gradually from agricultural products to the selling of antiques, bringing buyers from all over the world. In some ways the town could be said to be undiscovered and that certainly contributes to its attraction. A visit to the Tourist Information Office in quaint School Lane is certain to help you discover Leominster, which describes itself as the "Town which Time forgot".

Of all the places on the Black and White Trail, Leominster has the most public transport. British Rail has frequent services to the north through Shrewsbury, and to South Wales and Bristol via Hereford and Newport. Bus services to the west of the area covered by the Black and White Trail walk are more limited and it is essential that times are checked at the Bus Station before setting out. There is a full range of shops, several hotels and public houses, a main Post Office, Police Station and a Medical Centre.

Attractions Leominster is a town of considerable antiquity, being originally the site of an early religious foundation created by the Saxon King Merewald in 658 A.D. The first abbot of this tiny outpost of Christianity amid the pagan Celts was a Northumbrian monk called Ealfred. Later, in the ninth century, Lady Godiva's husband, Leofric, Earl of Mercia, endowed a nunnery here. It has been suggested that the Domesday Book name of the town, Leofminstre, refers to Leofric and the Minster.

Being a Border town, Leominster was subject to frequent assault, capture and recapture, by the warring factions of the Marches, whether Danes who came up the River Lugg in their longboats, Celts from Wales, or Saxons and Normans from the south and east.

It had one great asset which enabled it to rise again from each setback - wool - from the famous Rylands breed of sheep. The lustrous nature of the fleece gave it the name of "Lemster Ore" and on the sheeps' backs Leominster flourished. Its prosperity in early mediaeval times ensured its growth, and attracted occasional incursions from Wales. As late as 1405 a rebellion led by Owain Glyndwr successfully took the town and plundered it and the abbey. However, more peaceful years followed and the woollen trade regained its eminence.

THE MILL STREAM, EARDISLAND

From then on it was economic and political battles which shaped the course of the wool trade, such as in 1536 when Hereford and Worcester cities brought about the closure of Leominster's Saturday market. Worse still was to come with the Dissolution of the Monasteries and the closure of Leominster Abbey. As the principal landowner and employer of labour in the area the shutting down of the abbey must have been like the modern failure of a major company, plus the collapse of the Social Security system. The magnificent buildings were pulled down and had it not been for the townsfolk taking action there would have been little left of the abbey today. By building a wall across the naves and making an offer for what remained they retained all that part which forms the present Priory church. There also remains the Benedictine Prior's house, adjacent to the churchyard. Its size and solidity gives you some idea of what the whole complex of buildings must have been like originally.

Leominster townsfolk were always Royalist and after supporting Catholic Queen Mary Tudor against her Protestant rival Lady Jane Grey by wiping out all Lady Jane's local supporters, the town was rewarded by the Queen with its Charter of Incorporation in 1554. Nearly a century later the town's Royalist sympathies were again put to the test in the Civil War. Colonel John Birch (see Weobley) of the Parliamentary Army attacked the town in 1643 and captured it in three days.

However, the wool trade's days in Leominster were numbered with the onset of the Industrial Revolution. Like most of the West Country woollen towns, Leominster lost out to the new centres of Northern England and the trade declined until there was none. Nevertheless, as a market town in a well-favoured agricultural area new developments in farming enabled it to develop its market and farm-related industries.

Leominster welcomed the railway in the 1850's. In fact it became a busy junction at the centre of a rural network with branch lines to New Radnor. Presteigne and Bromyard. Gone are these fine Great Western Railway branches, but traces of them can still be seen on the Black and White Trail. It also continued to be a social centre, as witness the remaining fine Assembly Rooms.

Today Leominster faces considerable change in its agricultural base, as well as the dilemma of most small towns as to how to survive and prosper as a community. Even the passing visitor may sense that the community feeling is still there, not least of all in the friendliness of the townsfolk. As with all the places on this Trail, it pays to take your time to look and listen while you are there.

Leominster to Dilwyn

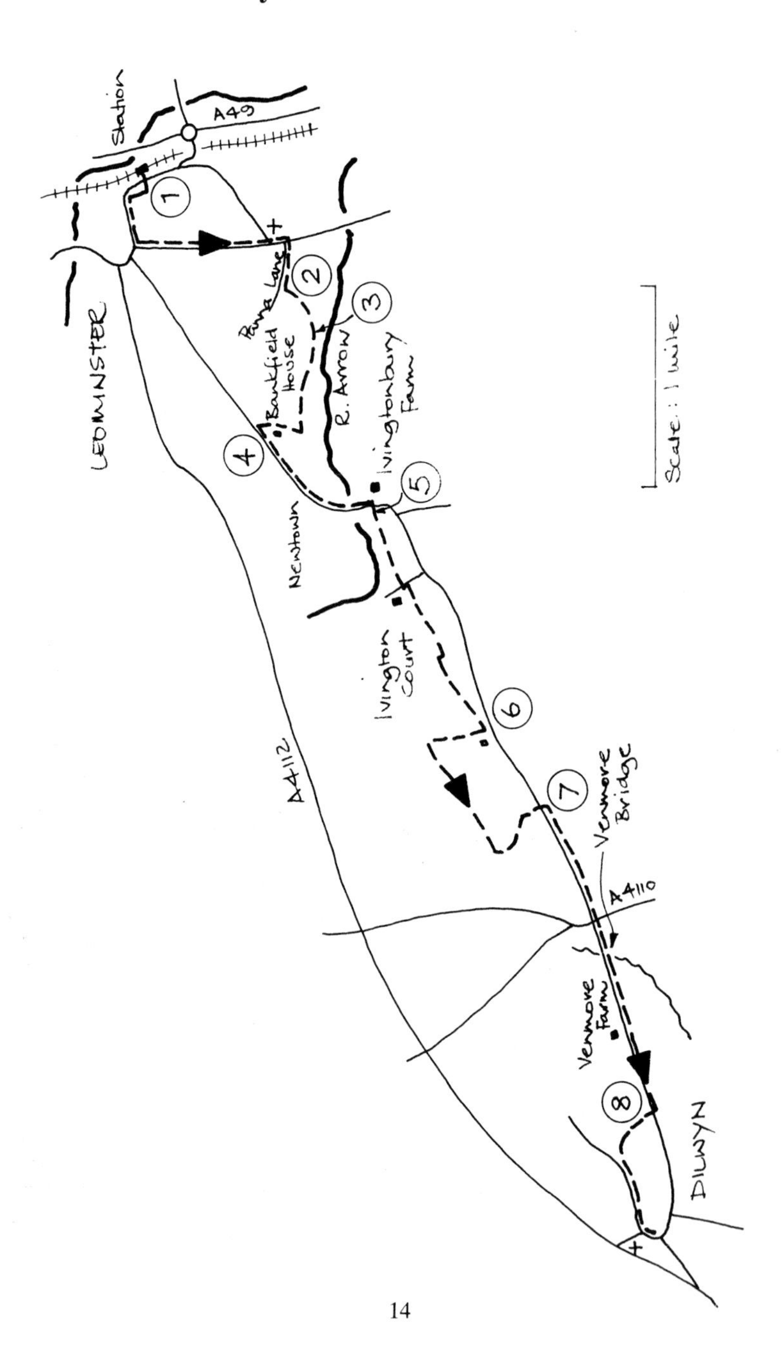

Black and White Trail — Section A

Leominster to Dilwyn — 12 miles

START *Leominster Railway Station.*

1 *Turn right out of the station forecourt and follow the road into Etnam St., a broad thoroughfare leading to a junction by the Royal Oak Hotel. Turn left here and follow the main road to a church and cemetery where you turn right into Passa Lane.*

2 *After the lane bends to the right by a building, turn left soon afterwards down a hedged track which leads to a barred gate. Go through it to the riverside meadow. Head right across the field to cross a stile into a large field.*

3 *Avoid the temptation of following the river bank, but walk slightly right towards a solitary tree as you climb the brow of the field. Keep ahead to a stile, with a wood now to your right. Cross the stile and the footbridge over the ditch before proceeding ahead, once again, to a gateway which allows access into a lane. Follow this to a tarmac road and turn left.*

4 *Follow the road to pass by houses at Newtown and then along a straight section (avoiding a turn to the right) continuing across the flood plain of the River Arrow. Once over the river bridge, look for a set of double gates opposite a long barn at Ivingtonbury Farm.*

5 *Go through the gate and walk ahead a short distance to a another barred gate. Make your way across a large field, heading to the left of Ivington Court. Cross a stile in a fence and keep ahead to another stile leading on to a track. Go left, walk a matter of thirty paces and turn right through a gateway into a field. Keep ahead with the field hedge to your left, through two further gateways eventually to meet a track crossing your path at the third. Go right on to it but then turn left before the hedge only to pass through a gap in it within several paces. Once through the gap keep ahead, now with the hedge on your left through another two gateways.*

6 *At the field corner (with houses just beyond) turn right and follow the field edge down at first but then cutting across right to a barred gate at the bottom of the field. Once through, bear left to cross a wooden barrier and keep ahead. Follow the fence to the corner, go left through the gate and then right, with a small plantation to your left. Head slightly right to pass through a gap beneath a large tree just to the right of the spinney. In the next field proceed ahead, once again, through a gateway beneath a large oak, and about twenty paces beyond the remnants of an old hedge, turn left to join the right hand field hedge. Follow the old green lane alongside this hedge up the hill through gateways to a barred gate which exits on to a road by a cottage.*

7 *Turn right here and follow this road to the main A4110 road which should be crossed with utmost care, turning right and then left into the Dilwyn road.*

8 *In half a mile, beyond Venmore Farm, look for a stile on the right leading into an orchard. Cross it and walk ahead to another stile leading into a pasture overlooking Dilwyn village. Walk ahead at first but then cross left to a stile in the bottom left corner. Go over this and follow the field's edge to a gateway in the corner. Follow the track to the road and turn left to walk into the village by the Post Office and then left by the church to the village green.*

LOCAL WALK

Dilwyn **6 miles**

Outline Dilwyn ~ Little Dilwyn ~ Alton Crossroads ~ Dilwyn.

Summary The walk is across fields to Little Dilwyn Farm returning by lanes and across gentle pastures. The paths are very old but have only recently been cleared for walkers so are easy to follow. There are no real climbs.

Attractions The village of Dilwyn is tucked into a wooded hollow, unseen until one is almost on top of it, so its Old English name, meaning a shady or secret place, is as appropriate today as it was a thousand years ago. Fortunately a by-pass built in 1973 diverts the traffic so that it is possible to stand in the middle of the village and take in its quiet beauty without risking an artic. in the back!

The village green has a magnificent cedar tree facing a row of cottage homes converted from one of the great Tithe barns that were built over 300 years ago to house the Tithes (taxes in kind) that every landholder had to pay to the Lord of the Manor and the Rector of the parish church of St. Mary the Virgin. On the way to the church from the green it is possible to see the other parts of the conversion - 19 spacious homes that have been skilfully incorporated into these great barns.

Like all the Marches villages, Dilwyn has not always been so peaceful and a hint of this can be noticed in the tiny slit windows of the church tower (c.1200), more suited to a castle keep than a church tower. The spire is a "recent" eighteenth century addition to the tower, presumably built for aesthetic purposes.

The church was closely connected with Wormsley Priory whose workmen built the present nave, chancel and porch at varying times during the 13th and 14th centuries. This has left a remarkably compact set of examples, best seen in the windows, of all the styles of mediaeval architecture from Early English, through Decorated to Perpendicular. Of about this time is the canopied tomb in the wall of the chancel with the figure of a knight in chain mail. It is thought that this person was a member of the Talbot family who founded Wormsley Priory. The other local family, the Delaberes, have their coat of arms, together with that of the Talbots, in the chancel windows.

Dilwyn is fortunate that its church registers have survived complete from 1558, offering a valuable key to family historians seeking their rural forbears. Another valuable key is the one to the door in the South Porch. At 17ins. (430 mm) long it must qualify, not only for the Guinness Book of Records, but as the least likely church door key in Herefordshire to be mislaid!

One of the church bells has the sobering inscription -

"I to the church the living call,
and to the grave do summon all"

Refreshments The Crown Inn, offering light snacks, is a welcome sight for the thirsty walker.

DILWYN CHURCH

Dilwyn

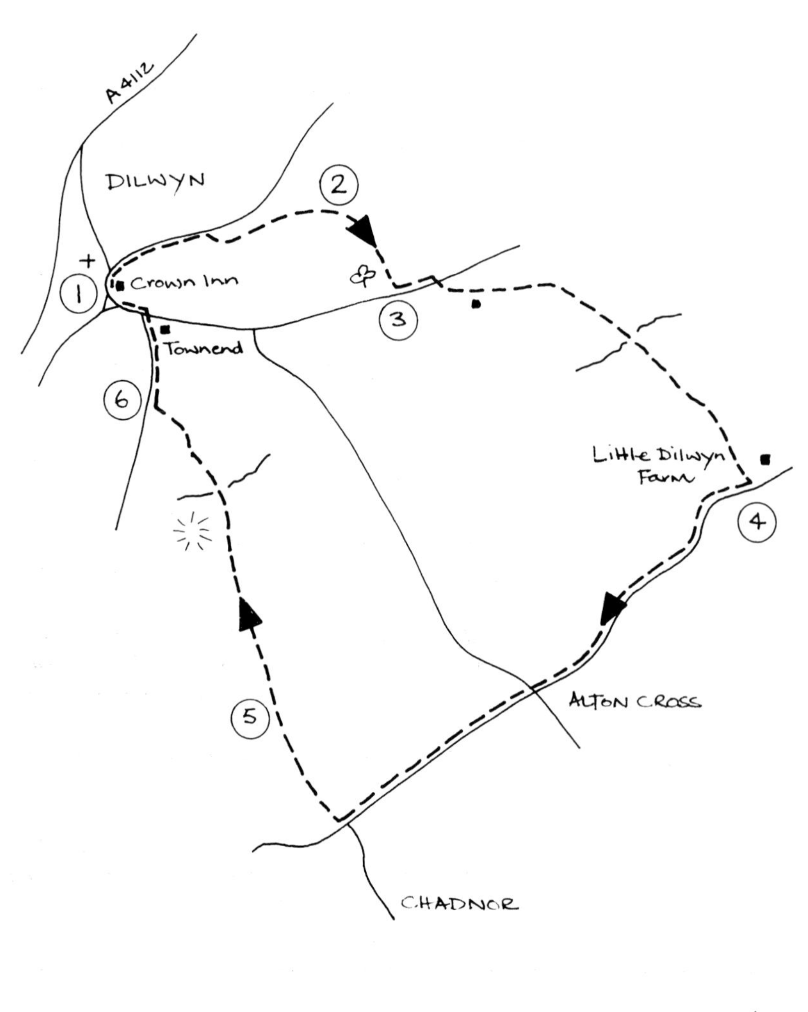

A4112
DILWYN
2
1
Crown Inn
3
Townend
6
Little Dilwyn Farm
4
5
ALTON CROSS
CHADNOR
Scale: 1 mile (1.6km)

LOCAL WALK

Dilwyn — 6 miles

START *The Crown Inn, Dilwyn*

1 *Turn right to pass the Dilwyn Stores and right again by the church. As the road bends left keep ahead to pass the Post Office and a telephone kiosk further along. Not far after, as the road curves to the left turn right up a track and go through a gate into the field. Bear left and follow the hedge on the left to a stile which you cross.*

2 *Walk a few paces forward and then bear slightly right up the hill to cross a stile in the top left hand corner to enter an orchard. Keep ahead to another stile which exits into a lane.*

3 *Turn left and then very shortly go through a barred gate on the right, as signed, and through the field to cross two stiles guarding a track. Keep ahead with the cottage to your right and cross a stile in the corner of the field. Keep to the hedge on the left for a hundred paces or so before striking out across the field, as waymarked, to a footbridge and stile in the hedge at the bottom. Keep ahead to another footbridge and then follow the hedgerow on the left until it begins to indent left. Proceed ahead from this point to the middle gate leading into an orchard by Little Dilwyn Farm. Go slightly right to pass through another gate and then slightly left to a stile which brings you into a lane by a sharp corner, so be wary of traffic.*

4 *Turn right and walk for the best part of a mile, straight ahead at Alton crossroads (or right if you require a shorter lane walk back to Dilwyn) and then at the next junction to Chadnor, turn right through the gate into a field, where there are good views across to Dilwyn. This field is often in crop but a path is usually left down the centre so proceed ahead along a narrow strip to cross a stile at the far end.*

5 *Keep ahead, once again, to cross another stile and go slightly right across a field with the earthworks of an ancient site to your left. Go over a footbridge and then keep company with the hedgerow on your right. Cross the stile and walk the short distance to a footbridge. Once over, go left along the field boundary to cross two stiles and join the Weobley road.*

6 *Turn right and at the junction by Townsend go left for the short distance to the village green.*

Dilwyn to Weobley

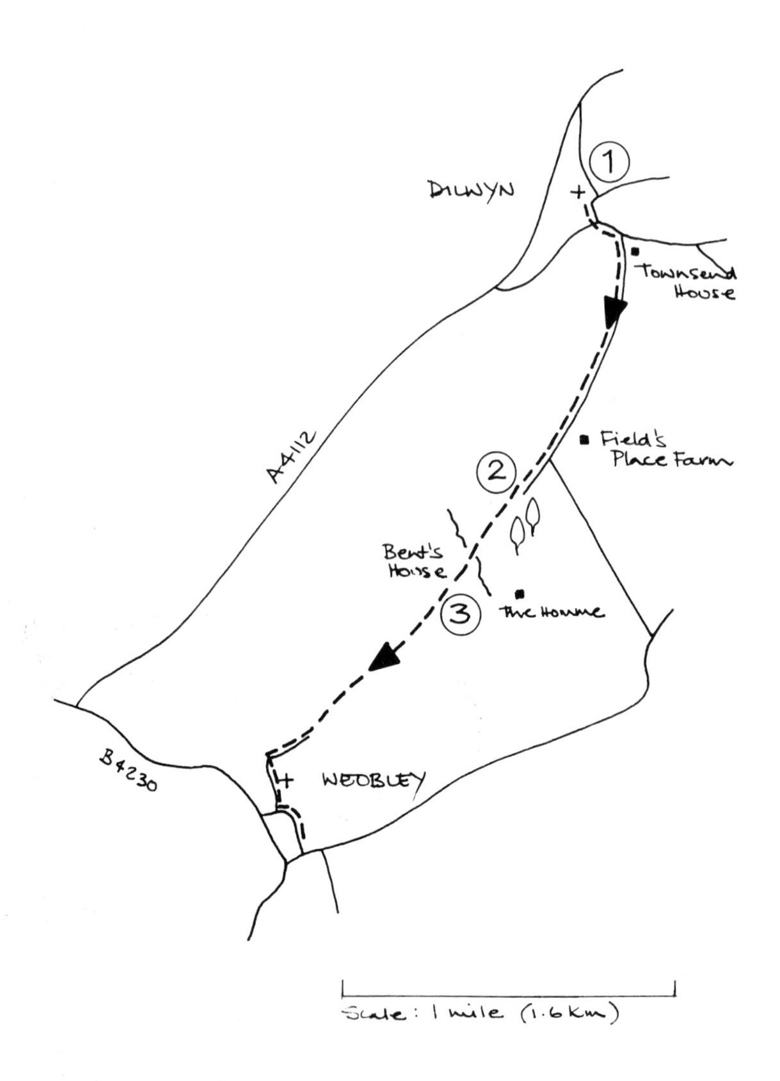

Black and White Trail — Section B

Dilwyn to Weobley — 3 miles

START *Dilwyn Village Stores.*

1 *From the Crown Inn turn left. Follow the road a short distance and turn right at the next junction by the impressive Townsend House. Walk along the road and as it climbs and turns left, with Fields Place Farm on the left, go ahead through the gateway as signed, into a field with the magnificent spire of Weobley church coming into sight.*

2 *The path passes alongside the wood on the left to a gate. Once through keep slightly right following the line of an old green track as it contours down between the oak trees to a bridge across the brook. Pass to the left of a barn and to another gate by the scant remains of Bent's House.*

3 *Follow the clear bridleway ahead through fields, with the spire of Weobley church as a directional guide. The path exits on to a lane by the church. Go right and then second left to pass by the church and then left into the centre of Weobley village. (If you are continuing on the trail, look for a stile on the right before the church. Cross this and follow the well worn path through this small paddock, across a footbridge and to a narrow passage beyond another stile leading on to the B4230 road where you turn right.).*

WEOBLEY

LOCAL WALK

Weobley — 3½ miles

Outline Weobley ~ Ledgemoor ~ Garnstone Park ~ Weobley.

Summary Village to common, parkland and castle mound, all within a matter of three miles. There are fine views from the old drive which at one time ran up to Garnstone Court, now a melancholy ruin. The views of Weobley church and beyond are splendid on a winter's day. A good walk mainly along paths and tracks with no real climbs.

Attractions For the traveller there is no doubt where Weobley (pronounced Webb-ly) is situated. The highest steeple of the parish church, dedicated to St. Peter and St. Paul, is a landmark that can be seen for miles around. Quite rightly, as it is the second highest in the county, a fact which caused less lofty minds to produce the rhyme about Weobley - "Low church, high steeple; poor place, proud people".

The strange spelling of Weobley harks back to its Saxon origins. Weobba's Ley possibly refers to its founding by a Mercian prince of that name in the Sixth century. The Normans literally reinforced its position when the de Lacy family built a castle there in the early twelfth century and made it their headquarters. The small settlement was sufficiently notable to be allowed to send two members to Parliament in the late thirteenth century, but lost this privilege in 1307 because its inhabitants refused to pay their M.P.s' expenses of two shillings a day. An early case of requiring value for money, one imagines! It seems that the inhabitants had to wait until 1628 before getting back their parliamentary rights which lasted until the Reform Act of 1832 removed Weobly as a "Rotten Borough" from the lists.

There are many fine timber-framed houses still standing but here would have been even more had not the Marquis of Bath, the local landowner, pulled at least forty down in the 1820s. A further blow came in 1943 when a disastrous fire in the Market Place destroyed all the remaining buildings in the middle of the street, leaving an empty space now occupied by a small ornamental garden and bus shelter. The style and size of the old houses indicates the prosperity of Weobley which, although always a market town, developed a successful glove-making industry in the seventeenth and eighteenth centuries. This reached its peak in the early nineteenth century during the Napoleonic Wars when it became impossible to obtain gloves from France, the traditional source.

It had its own Grammar School, founded as a free school in about 1659 and the building, now a private residence, can be seen on the Hereford Road, just round the corner from the "Unicorn". If the original Market Hall had been retained, it would have been the most impressive building in the village, matched at least in human interest by the adjacent Mansion House where, in one room in the latter half of the sixteenth century, thirty-three children were born by two women to James Tonkins. They all lived and so caused a local poet to pen three verses about this remarkable achievement - the last will suffice:

"And may the loud resounding trump of fame,
Proclaime great Tomkins for a man of men.
In golden letters, O!, engrave his name
In marble tablets with an iron pen.
Let this survive this house and last when all
Its beams doe tremble and the rafters fall".

The church, the third at least on this site, is mainly Decorated and Perpendicular in style with fragments of the earlier buildings incorporated. It is a fine structure and contains some interesting memorials to the early Weobley families such as the Devereux and Marburys whose fifteenth century tombs are found in the Chancel.

Closer to the altar is a memorial to Col. Birch, one of Cromwell's loyal officers, who captured Leominster during the English Civil War. In 1661 he bought a fine house called Garnstone, about half a mile out of the village, and turned it into a mansion. After the Restoration of Charles II, however, he became the very model of a Royalist supporter, providing the funds for the restoration of the church spire in 1675 after it had begun to fall down, and generally behaving in the approved manner of a country gentleman!

One wonders if he ever thought about that night in September 1645 when, after the battle of Naseby, King Charles I took temporary refuge in one of the Weobley houses, now called the Throne.

Sad to say, Garnstone Castle, as it became after rebuilding by Nash in 1807, was pulled down in 1959, although the Lodges to the Estate still exist.

There is much of interest to be found in the small village Museum and, if you are lucky you may be able to find a copy of the Guide to the village to help you to better appreciate the remarkable old buildings and the stories that lie behind them.

Accommodation and Refreshments Weobley is well provided with accommodation in small guest houses and the pubs. There is a small high-quality restaurant as well as good restaurants in several of the pubs. A short walk around the centre of the village will provide some idea of the choice available.

There is a branch of Lloyds Bank (open daily except Wednesdays), and a Post Office (shut on Wednesday and Saturday afternoons).

Public Transport There are regular bus services to Hereford and Kington on weekdays, and a limited service to Leominster. Timetable information is available.

Weobley

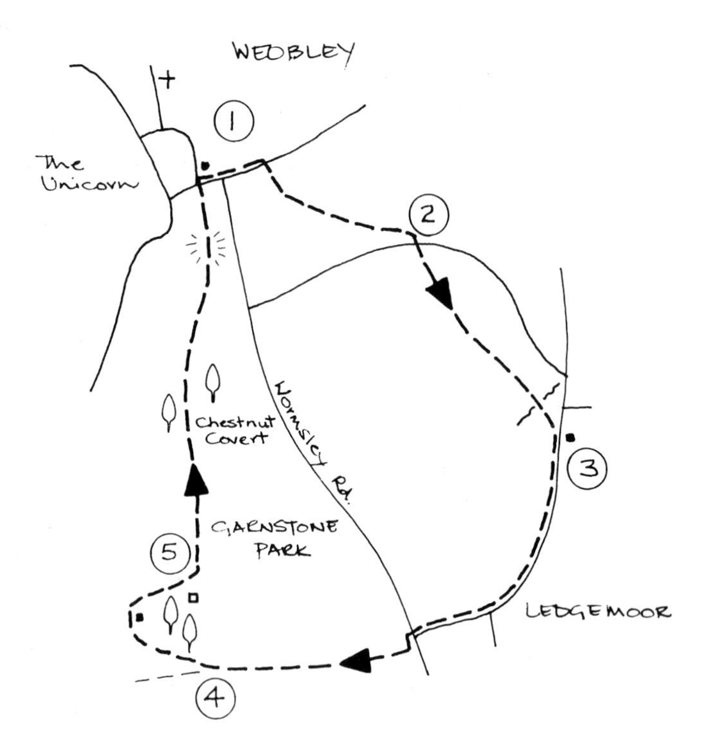

WEOBLEY
1
The Unicorn
2
Chestnut Covert
Wormsley Rd.
3
GARNSTONE PARK
5
LEDGEMOOR
4
Scale: 1 mile / 1.6km

LOCAL WALK

Weobley **5 miles**

START *From the Unicorn Inn, Weobley.*

1 *Turn left and as the Wormsley road bears right walk ahead along the lane signed to Dilwyn. Just past the dental surgery on the right go right along a surfaced path by small bungalows and then into a track curving left. Cross the bars on the right to enter the field and then go slightly left, through the gap into an orchard and left to a stile which you cross. Head for the far right corner and cross the stile into the lane.*

2 *Go over the road and then turn right up a green track which soon enters a field. Follow the hedge on the right ahead through two gateways and still ahead with the hedge now on your left. This soon drops away to the left but your way is ahead and then slightly left with a cottage in the background. Cross a footbridge and stile and make your way to a gateway to the right of the cottage which exits into a lane.*

3 *Turn right and follow the lane through Ledgemoor avoiding turns to the left. You come to a junction with the Wormsley road where you turn left and then right into Garnstone Park. Use the stiles to the left of the gates and then walk along the track passing a number of gates. Look out for the views of the ruined Garnstone Court to your right and shortly the main track will bear left uphill.*

4 *However, keep ahead to cross a stile, with signpost, and bear right across the field to a vintage iron kissing gate. Go through it and proceed to a stile just to the left of the walled garden. Cross the track and go through the barred gate into parkland once again. This leads right and in the field corner you catch another glimpse of the ruins which are not open to the public.*

5 *Turn left here to follow what was at one time a more important drive through parkland with an excellent view of Weobley church. After the second gate the path heads slightly right to the remains of Weobley castle. In fact the path passes through the earthworks and along a lane to return to the Unicorn.*

Weobley to Almeley

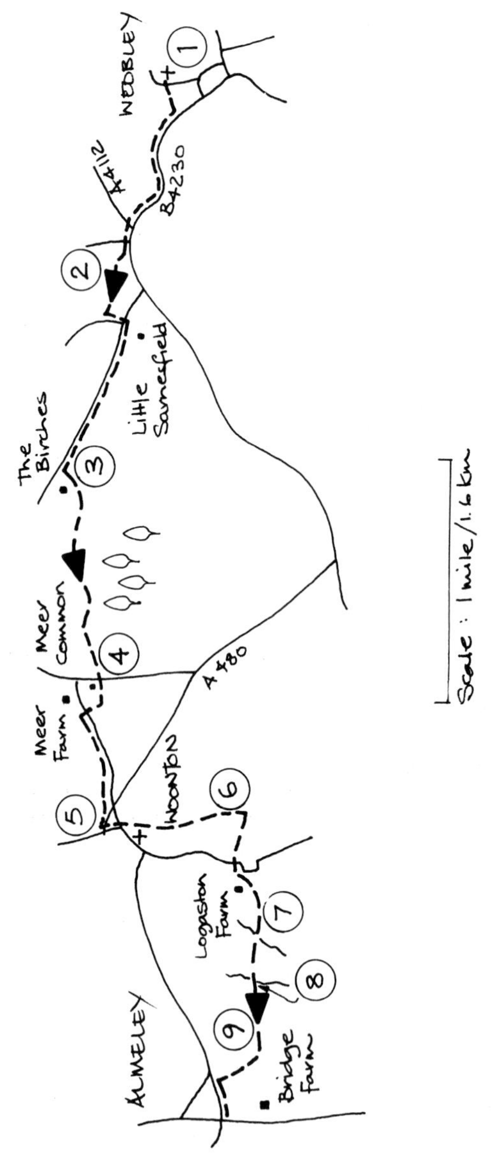

9 *Keep ahead in this field but look for a stile on the right. Cross it and follow the field boundary on the left up to cross another stile. Walk ahead once again to cross a stile leading on to a tarmac road. Turn left for Almeley village and right at the junction by the church.*

Black and White Trail **Section C**

Weobley to Almeley **8 miles**

START *Weobley village centre.*

1 *From Weobley village head in the direction of the church and turn left to join the main B4230. Turn right and follow this road to its junction with the A4112. Cross at the junction and keep ahead to pass by the garage on the right. As the road turns left go through a gateway to the left of a red brick cottage which leads into a field.*

2 *Walk slightly to the right, up the field, to go through another gateway (on the right) and track. Head slightly right to cross a stile in the top right corner of the field into a lane. Turn left and follow this lane a short distance to a junction where you turn right. Follow the lane for about one quarter of a mile.*

3 *Turn left along the tarmac lane leading to the Birches Farm. However, look for the second gate on the left before the farm which leads down to a stile. Cross this and then keep ahead over a drainage ditch and to a gate by the wood. Go through it and proceed ahead to another gate. Go through it and head right to the corner of the wood. Follow the perimeter of the wood to the next field boundary where you go through the gate on the left and then a gate on the right. Keep ahead along the field's edge to a broken gate exiting on to the road.*

4 *Go a few paces left, cross the road and go through the gate. Go left through another gate and head slightly right to the field corner where you cross a stile. Keep company with the hedge on the right to exit shortly through a gate on to a tarmac road at Meer Common. Turn left and follow this into Woonton, joining the main A480 road. Cross the road, walk a very short distance before turning left along a lane.*

5 *At the Friends Meeting House (dating from 1888) turn left along a track. Before reaching the barred gate go right over a stile hidden underneath trees. Walk ahead to the corner of the field and then go left, now proceeding down the field with the hedge to your right.*

6 *Go through the gateway and keep ahead until you come to the far right corner of the field where you cross the stile into an old green lane and turn right. Come to a tarmac road at Logaston and keep ahead. As this road veers left after a farm and cottage proceed ahead through a wide gateway and after a short section, with Logaston Farm to your right, follow the green lane which leads gently right at the fork in the tracks.*

7 *This descends gently through two gateways and to a stream. Soon it comes to the earth remains of a one-time substantial hedge. Go to the left of the hedge and keep ahead in this large field with the hedge now to your right.*

8 *At the corner look for a path which slopes down the bank to a footbridge and then climb up into another large field, a solitary tree being your directional guide. Your way should be slightly left to cross a wire fence and then to a footbridge and stile in the next boundary. As the fence is obstructing the route keep ahead to go through three barred gates in succession heading towards Bridge Farm in the distance.*

LOCAL WALK

Almeley

6 miles

Outline Almeley ~ The Batch ~ Hopsley Green ~ Woonton ~ Logaston ~ Almeley.

Summary A varied walk between the village of Almeley and Woonton mainly using local paths and tracks between the two settlements. There are good views over the Merbach range to the Black Mountains.

Attractions In 1086 King William of Normandy's scribes wrote down the name of this village as "Elmelie", which was as near as they could get to its old Saxon name of "Elmeleah" - the Elmwood. It would be very difficult to find any living elms in Almeley today, but there is a fine selection of very old timbered buildings dating from the twelfth to the seventeenth centuries. Most visitors' eyes are caught by the lovely fifteenth century Manor House close by the church, but perhaps the oldest and finest timber structure in the village is at Castle Froome Farm. Here it is not the house but the barn which is of the greater antiquity and architectural interest. It is likely that this is the original early mediaeval farm house, and its great cruck beams date back to the early thirteenth century, if not before.

A building as old as this in such a position must have seen times of excitement, anxiety and relief centred round the mound, or "Toot", which is close by. This relic of a small, timber-built fort, together with another later one called Oldcastle Toot above the Batch, shows that this part of the border land needed a vigilant defence from time to time. The latter castle was the home of Sir John Oldcastle, famous Lollard and follower of Wycliffe, a dissenting religious leader. Sir John was imprisoned in the Tower for his beliefs in 1413, escaped to the border country and was eventually recaptured in Montgomeryshire. It is thought that Shakespeare based his Sir John Falstaff on Almeley's Sir John.

The mainly fourteenth century St. Mary's church has an unusual Tudor painted roof and a tower with massive walls, hinting at its function as a refuge in times of turmoil. Just outside the village is a much later religious refuge founded by the Quakers in 1672. The Meeting House, still in use, was built by Roger Pritchard who owned Summer House Farm nearby. The name of the farm harks back to earlier days when Welsh was spoken almost as much as English in this area, and when this was a Hafod, a place to which the cattle were brought in summer for grazing. The farmhouse sits in a delightful setting and is a charming mixture of stone, brick and timber.

By the beginning of this century much of the land around Almeley had become part of the Nieuport Estate, but this was sold off in 1909 and a large part re-sold in 1919 when the fine Nieuport House became a sanatorium. This in its turn was bought by the Latvian Society in 1953 as a home for Latvian refugees who could not return to their homeland. At Midsummer Night each year a great gathering of Latvian families living in this country takes place here, and the evening air tingles with the emotion of their singing.

Refreshment The Bells Inn is close to the church.

ALMELEY MANOR

Almeley

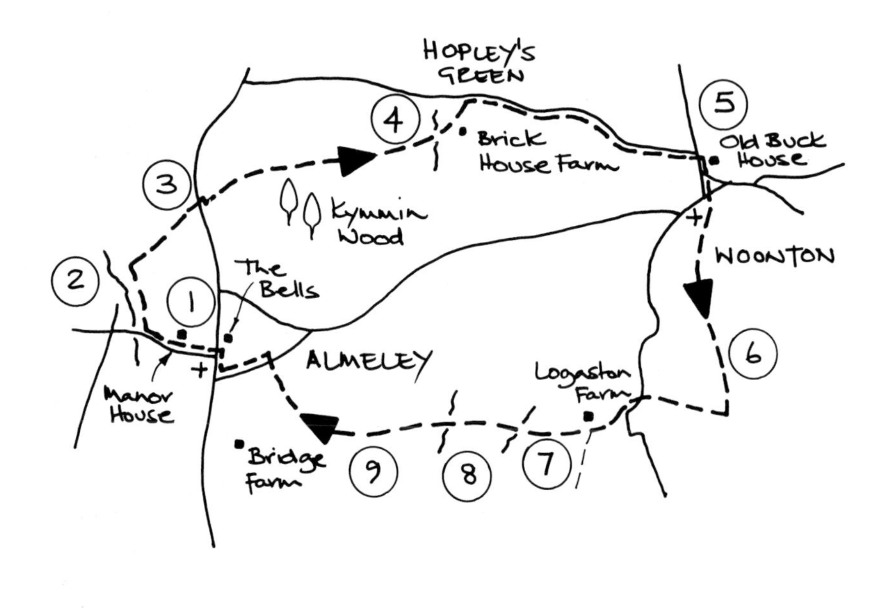

9 *Keep ahead in this field but look for a stile on the right. Cross it and follow the field boundary on the left up to cross another stile. Walk ahead once again to cross a stile leading on to a tarmac road. Turn left for Almeley village and right at the junction by the church.*

LOCAL WALK

Almeley **6 miles**

START *From the Bells public house.*

1 *Turn left and then before the church turn right to pass by the ancient manor house. As the road curves right as it dips towards the stream known as Letton Lake, go right along an access road to Batch cottage in the woodland. But within a matter of one hundred paces go right into the wood along a not too clearly identified path.*

2 *As you begin to climb, however, the path becomes well trodden. Go over the stile and keep ahead to cross over the lower level of fencing into a field. Go right alongside the hedge at first but then cut slightly left across the field to a stile by two trees. Cross here and head slightly left again to a gate by a garden which brings you into a tarmac lane.*

3 *Turn right for a few steps and then turn left over a stile. Head slightly left and cross another stile by a gate. Then walk slightly right towards Kymmin wood, keeping ahead along the wood's edge to cross a stile in the corner of the field. Go ahead across this next enclosure to another stile which is not seen immediately. Cross it and keep ahead again (although some local walkers prefer to turn right over a stile and then left along the track) to exit on to the track by a stream.*

4 *Keep ahead through Hopley's Green, passing Brick House Farm, to join a tarmac lane where you turn right. Follow this into the village of Woonton, keeping right at the T-junction by Tan House Cottage.*

5 *At the main road turn right by Old Buck House (at one time a pub) and right again to pass a telephone kiosk. At the T-junction cross the road and walk to the left of the Friends Meeting House (dating from 1888) along a track. Before reaching the barred gate go right over a stile hidden underneath trees, walk ahead to the corner of the field and then go left, now proceeding down the field with the hedge to your right.*

6 *Go through the gateway and keep ahead until you come to the far right corner of the field where you cross the stile into an old green lane and turn right. Come to a tarmac road and turn left. As this road veers left after a farm and cottage keep ahead through a wide gateway and after a short section, with Logaston Farm to your right, follow the green lane which leads gently right at the fork in the tracks.*

7 *This descends gently through two gateways and to a stream. Soon it comes to the earth remains of a one time substantial hedge. Go to the left of the hedge and keep ahead in this large field with the hedge now to your right.*

8 *At the corner look for a path which slopes down the bank to a footbridge and then climb up into another large field, a solitary tree being your directional guide. Your way should be slightly left to cross a wire fence and then to a footbridge and stile in the next boundary. As the fence is obstructing the route keep ahead to go through three barred gates in succession heading towards Bridge Farm in the distance.*

Almeley to Eardisley

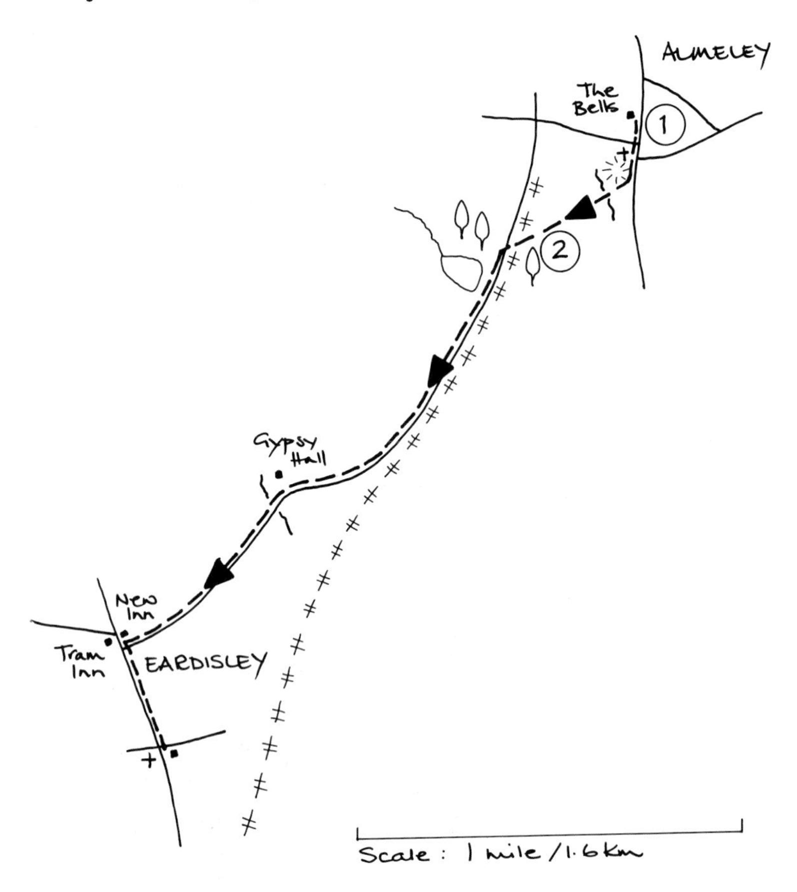

Black and White Trail — Section D

Almeley to Eardisley — 3 miles

START *The Bells public house, Almeley.*

1 *From the Bells public house turn left and pass to the left of the church as the lane descends. Cross a stile on the right and walk to the left of the motte and bailey mound to cross a stile and a stream. Keep slightly left and then ahead to another stile and then across another small field to an orchard.*

2 *Go through the orchard and through trees growing tall on the old railway line to a narrow strip of pasture and the Eardisley road. Turn left and follow this road for a mile into Eardisley village to the Tram and New inns on the main road. Turn left to walk through the village to the church.*

THE GREAT OAK, EARDISLEY

LOCAL WALK

Eardisley — 3 miles

Outline Eardisley church ~ The Park ~ Woodseaves Brook ~ The Great Oak ~ Hobby Lyons.

Summary A gentle walk across fields to the Great Oak of Eardisley. Good views across to the mountains of Wales.

Attractions It is said by its older inhabitants that Eardisley is the perfect village. If pressed for reasons they reply that when one enters the village from the Hereford direction one finds Salvation on the left and Education on the right - and on leaving from the other end of Eardisley's single street one can enjoy Damnation on both sides! It's not such a bad guide to follow their approved route and begin with Salvation.

The church of St. Mary Magdalene has been a place of worship since the early twelfth century and set within its solid walls is a gem of Romanesque art. This is its font which dates from around 1130. The group of stonemasons who shaped it had a unique style, incorporating elements of Celtic, Saxon and Norman-French tradition as well as being influenced by the carvings found in the Spanish pilgrimage cathedral of Santiago de Compostela. The figures around the sides of the font represent the well-known mediaeval religious theme of the Harrowing of Hell, or the saving of a sinner from the toils of the Devil, who is represented as a lion. In this case, though, there is a unique addition to the traditional representation - two armed men fighting. It now seems very probable that this refers to a violent incident in the life of Ralph de Baskerville, Lord of the Manor of Eardisley, who around 1126 killed his father-in-law in single combat in order to settle a dispute over land. This event brought about a complete change in Ralph's lifestyle, which had all sorts of repercussions locally, one of which was probably the commissioning of this font with its visual message of redemption.

There is little left to see of Eardisley's warlike past. The Castle, which once housed a Bishop of Hereford in its dungeons, and which fought off invading Welsh armies, has gone, except for its central mound and traces of its moats. The last remnants were burned down in the English Civil War in 1645 and a charming Georgian farmhouse now stands on the site.

Another fine eighteenth century house can be seen by taking the small road beside the church and following the village walk. Soon after leaving the woodland surrounding the Castle Farm the house known as "The Park" is seen. The family that built the house, the Barnsleys, were involved in extremely lengthy legal proceedings over their inheritance which had been fraudulently denied them. It is said that their case, lasting 34 years in Chancery, gave Charles Dickens the inspiration for his novel, "Bleak House".

After glancing at Education (fortunately for the village the school is still open) a gentle stroll through the village will enable the visitor to look at the remarkable assortment of half-timbered houses. Quite a number of them were once single farmhouses and are now divided into three or four dwellings. Most date from the sixteenth or seventeenth centuries, although there are at least three which originate from the fourteenth century, their distinctive cruck beam construction indicating their great age.

On arrival at Tram Square, where "Damnation" is said to stand on each side, a road leads off to Woodseaves. Following this for about a mile past the fourteenth century Cruck House, the visitor will come upon the Eardisley Great Oak, tucked in behind a grey stone chapel. A landmark on maps in 1614, it is thought to be over 800 years old. It is hollow inside, having survived an internal fire in the 1950s, but is still capable of putting out a fine show of leaves and acorns each year.

Tram Square itself owes its name to the horse-drawn tramway which came to Eardisley in 1818 from Brecon, bringing cheap Welsh coal and taking back corn and lime. Long before that the Square was the market place in which a weekly market was held from 1262 onwards, and in which the hiring fairs took place annually right up until the 1920's.

Accommodation Eardisley is a good place to stay although it will not be immediately apparent that there are any places offering accommodation. It is the original village of Country Village Weekend Breaks and as such can offer very good B & B. An advance call to the Cruck House, (tel: 054-46-529), can ensure that this is arranged promptly.

Refreshment There are two public houses at Tram Square, the New Inn and the Tram, which offer bar snacks and light meals. The Central Stores will prepare instant rolls with fillings while you wait.

Eardisley has a Post Office, shut on Thursday and Saturday afternoons, and a branch of Barclay's Bank open on Fridays.

There are buses on weekdays to Hereford and Kington, and to Hay-on-Wye on Thursdays. Times are shown on the Parish Notice Board by the Village Hall.

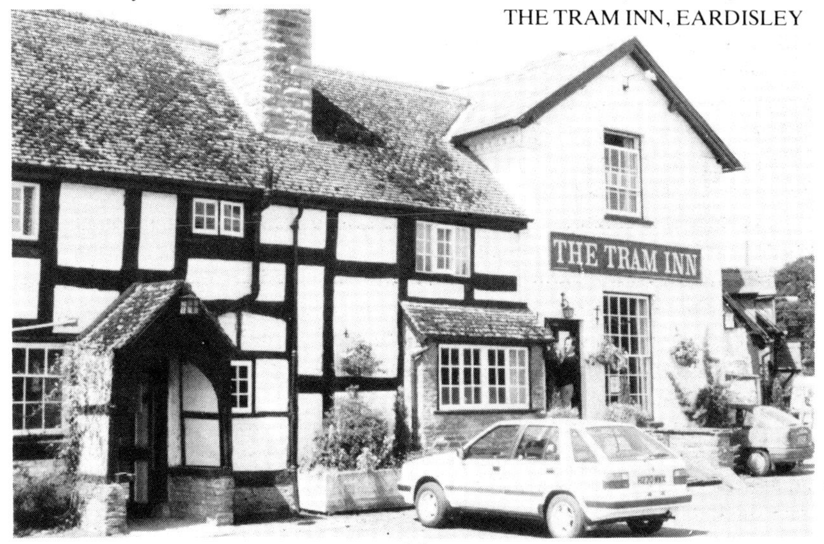

THE TRAM INN, EARDISLEY

Eardisley

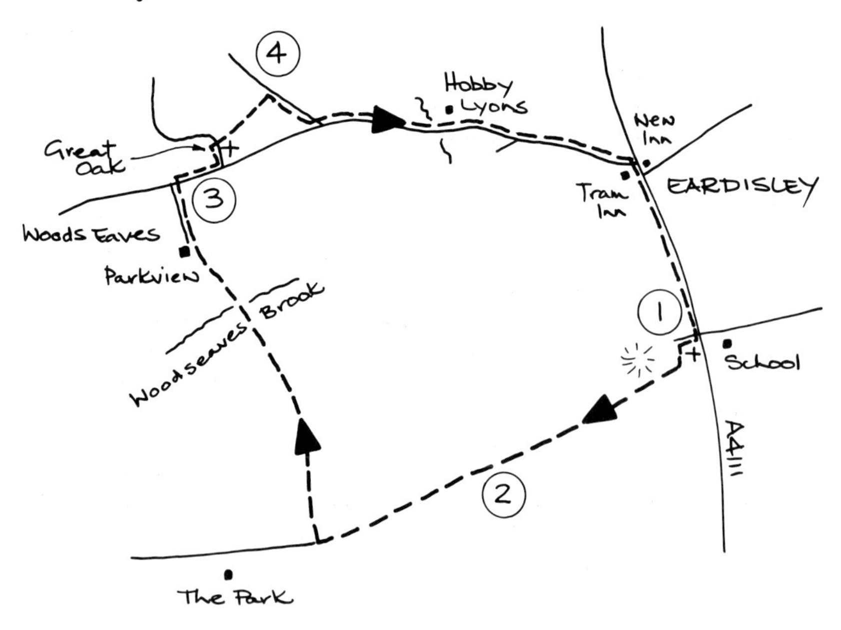

4
Hobby
Lyons
Great
Oak
New
Inn
EARDISLEY
Tram
Inn
3
Woods Eaves
Parkview
Woodseaves Brook
1
School
A4111
2
The Park
Scale: 1 mile/1.6km

LOCAL WALK

Eardisley **3 miles**

START *At Eardisley Church.*

1 *Enter the churchyard by the Lych-gate, passing the church porch and exiting on to a track by a kissing gate. Bear left along the lane passing through the Castle copse before coming out on to open fields, across which there is a wonderful view of the Black Mountains to the south-west.*

2 *After a quarter of a mile "The Park" comes into view. Just before reaching the house turn right over a stile. Follow along the line of the right-hand hedge of this field, White Gate Field, passing through a small gate into Lower Tynings and then Cowbitch Meadow, alongside the Woodseaves Brook. Cross the Brook by the plank bridge, keeping the hedge on your right. Make for the fieldgate next to the house - Parkview. A metalled lane leads from there to a junction with the Woodseaves road.*

3 *Turn right and after two cottages turn left beside the old Fundamentalist Methodist chapel to reach the Great Oak, the oldest living inhabitant of the parish! Enter the small gate into the Chapel graveyard behind the Oak. Leave by the far right corner into a field. Keep to the left-hand hedge of two fields and exit through a fieldgate on to a lane.*

4 *Turn right along the lane, shortly rejoining the Woodseaves road at "The Turn". Bear left, crossing the brook at Hobby Lyons and coming out at Tram Square. Turn right through the village past many Black and White houses, to reach the Church Lych-gate again.*

NOTE: This walk can be taken in the opposite direction, starting at Tram Square and going up the road marked "Woodseaves" to the left of the inn. After heavy rain the fields near to the Woodseaves Brook can be muddy, but the route is rarely impassable to those wearing sensible footwear.

Eardisley to Kington

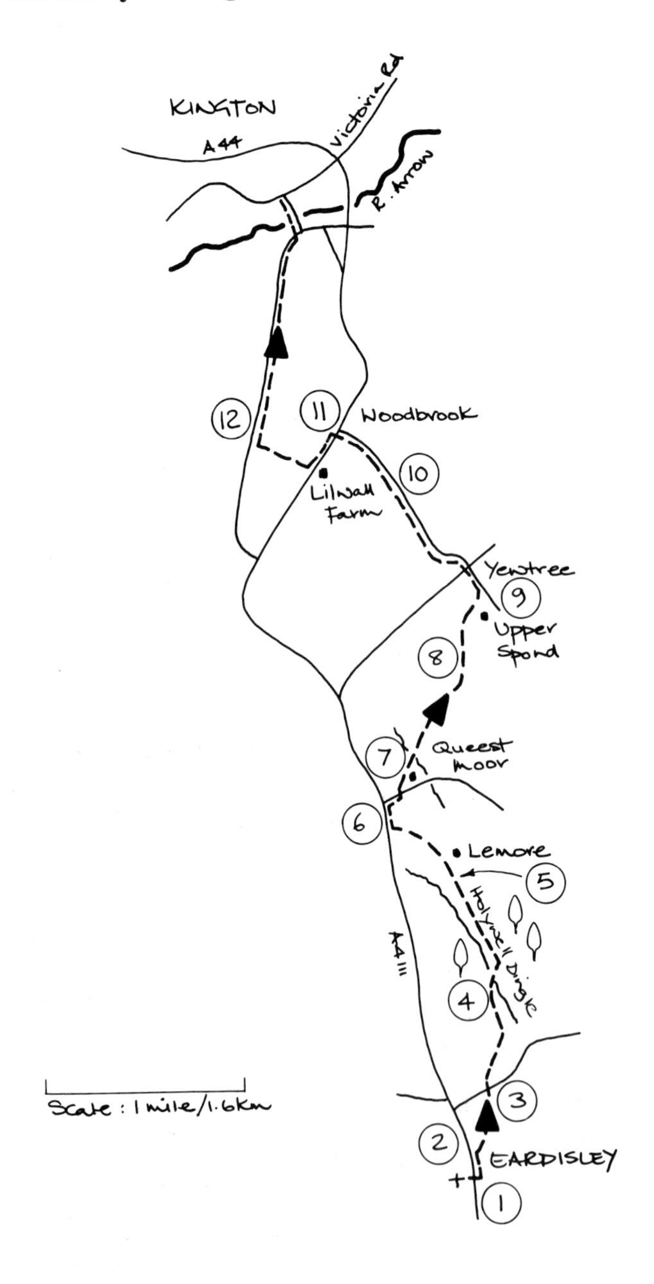

Black and White Trail — Section E

Eardisley to Kington — 9 miles

START *Eardisley church.*

1 *From Eardisley church, cross the main road and turn left. Pass the telephone kiosk and go right. The path leads across the field slightly left and between hawthorns into the next field.*

2 *Go diagonally right to the corner to cross a stile, a metal gate and then keep ahead along the raised old tramway route with bramble and rosehip bushes on either side. This exits by way of a high stile on to the Almeley road.*

3 *Cross the road and go through the gate to the right of the house. Follow the field boundary on your right as it curves gently right. As the field begins to narrow, however, look for a gate on the opposite side of the field. Go through it and walk ahead, i.e. to the right of the line of trees.*

4 *At the head of the field turn right down the bank between the healthy looking gorse bushes and cross the brook. Go through the small gate and follow the well-used path up the bank and then to the left through the wood, waymarked with blue spots. You will soon come to a junction. Do not go left along the main path here but ahead to a small gate which leads into a field with Lemore beyond it.*

5 *Head for the barred gate to the left of the house. Go through it and follow the track as it bends left and then right around the perimeter of the gardens and on to a lane which passes a bungalow and eventually meets the main A4111 road.*

6 *Turn right and, after a very short distance, right again along the road to Almeley. Look for the stile on the left. Cross it and another ahead to meet a garden hedge. Follow this to another stile. Cross this and follow the hedge on the right to a stile leading into a thicket.*

7 *Keep ahead to the left of the stream for a short distance, go through a gate and cross the stream by way of a covered bridge. Follow a hedge on the right to the field corner where you cross a stile. Continue ahead through a gateway and in the corner of the field cross the wooden bars into a field on the right. Keep ahead to cross an old gateway and in the next field, walk into the dip where you go through the gateway.*

8 *Once through, turn left and walk up this narrow pasture to go through the gateway ahead avoiding the one nearby on the right. Cut across the next field heading for the top right corner in the direction of the farm and go through the gateway in the thick hedge. Proceed up the field to the barbed wire fence and go through the gateway mid-way along it heading in a direction just to the left of the farm. Turn right on to the track. As it dips look for a stile and climb up the bank into the field. Walk diagonally across the field to the barred gate in the far corner.*

9 *At the lane, turn left and keep ahead at Yewtree crossroads. Follow the lane for a short while and at the junction take the path along the sunken lane on the right. This comes to an old gate which you go through and then turn right to cross another gate in a poor condition, re-joining the route of the ancient lane.*

10 *This delightful lane climbs gently at first and then descends more steeply to join another lane. Go left and follow the track to the main A4111 road at Woodbrook.*

continued on page 41

LOCAL WALK

Kington 4 miles

Outline Wordsworth's house ~ Hergest Croft Gardens ~ Haywood Common ~ Hergest Mill.

Summary A superb ramble passing places of great historic interest. Several climbs but easy to follow route.

Attractions All the villages and towns of the Marches have many characterful houses, but it seems that Kington also has had many "characters" as well. Some would say that this is still the case! Maybe it has been because of the mixing of Welsh and English blood here ever since Offa, King of Mercia, built his Dyke through the Kington area in the eighth century. The settlement known as "Kingtown", or Chingtune as it appears in the Domesday Book came much later when the future King Harold established the King's town not long before 1066.

From then on its border position presupposed strong characters to hold it and the Vaughan family fitted the bill very well. They lived at Hergest Court which is just outside the town and in the early Middle Ages it was also a centre of Welsh culture. Two of the most famous members of the family, Ellen and Thomas Vaughan, have their tomb in the Vaughan Chapel in Kington parish church, which is on the hill overlooking the present-day Kington, known originally as Kington in the Fields.

Thomas, or Black Vaughan, as he became known, caused as much trouble after his death as during his life, as he was given to appearing as a black dog, or bull, at the most inconvenient moments, scaring horses, animals and the inhabitants of Kington. Eventually a posse of thirteen clerics was assembled with their bells, books and candles and Black Vaughan's spirit was laid to rest in a silver snuffbox at the bottom of Hergest Pool. Things returned to normal until new owners at the Court unwittingly drained the Pool, found the snuffbox, opened it and let Black Vaughan out again! This time the religious round-up secured the wandering spirit under a large oak tree on the Hergest Estate, but only for a limited time which ended at the beginning of this century. There have been sightings since one in 1988!

This latter occasion did not include the regular voice from the tomb in the churchyard where one of the old drovers used to sleep in warm weather. He had the habit of enquiring the time of people passing by, especially in the early hours. Most were struck dumb on the first experiencing this sepulchral voice!

Other notable people who lived in Kington are the actress Sarah Siddons who made her stage debut in the town, and her brother Stephen Kemble of theatrical fame. William Wordsworth had a house called "Bywell" at Crooked Well and planted the fine Scots Pine in its garden. James Watt was a member of the Kington Tramroad Company that brought the Eardisley-Brecon Tramway to Kington in 1820. This caused the setting up of a local foundry which went on to be the basis of a sizeable local industry right up until the 1920's. The Kington laundry is on the site of the foundry near one of the roundabouts on the by-pass.

The Great Western Railway came and went leaving only traces of its tracks and buildings where the Industrial Estate is today. It is possible to trace its track and that of part of the Tramroad from near the Laundry to Floodgates, paralleling the bypass on the opposite side of the Back Brook.

When walking through the Kington Streets look up at the parts of the buildings above the shop fronts. Many of the smaller houses are half-timbered and there are some impressive buildings such as the ex-Kington Bank (now the Library) on the corner of Bridge Street and the old Assembly Rooms across the junction from it (now a Building Society office).

There is an excellent small Museum near the Victorian redbrick Market Hall at the western end of the town and a Tourist Information Centre nearby. Hergest Croft Gardens, at the home of the famous botanical Banks family, are open from April to October and can be reached by going up Church Street, past the church, bearing right and then taking the Ridgebourne Road on the left until the Gardens are reached.

The Kington Golf Course, reputedly the highest in the Kingdom, is at 100 ft. up on Bradnor Hill overlooking the town and the views can be breathtaking in more senses than one! The Club House can be reached by following the Offa's Dyke Path signs from the town, crossing first the Back Brook, then the bypass, and climbing the steep side of Bradnor.

Accommodation and Refreshment Kington is well provided with places to stay, from B & B to hotel, but at busy times in the season it is as well to book ahead through the Tourist Office. Its position on the Offa's Dyke long-distance path means that there is a steady demand for B & B accommodation from Spring to Autumn.

As for refreshment there are plenty of interesting pubs and small hotels offering everything from five-course meals to bar snacks. The town also has a number of cafes and take-aways.

The Post Office is at the junction of Bridge Street and High Street and there are branches of Barclays and Midland Banks.

Section E continued

11 *Cross the road with care and turn left. Walk up to a point just beyond the turning on the other side for Lilwall Farm. Go right through the next gateway by the Z bends road sign. Go through another gateway and then cross a stile in the corner of the field by the water trough. Continue ahead with the hedge on the right and cross three stiles to eventually come out on a tarmac road.*

12 *Turn right to descend for a mile into Kington joining the main road, once again by two toll houses. Go left and follow the road into town. If not visiting Kington, turn right after the River Arrow bridge along a signed footpath. Cross the stile by Tan House and then very shortly turn left into Love Lane to pass by the market. Turn right at the end on to Victoria Road.*

Kington

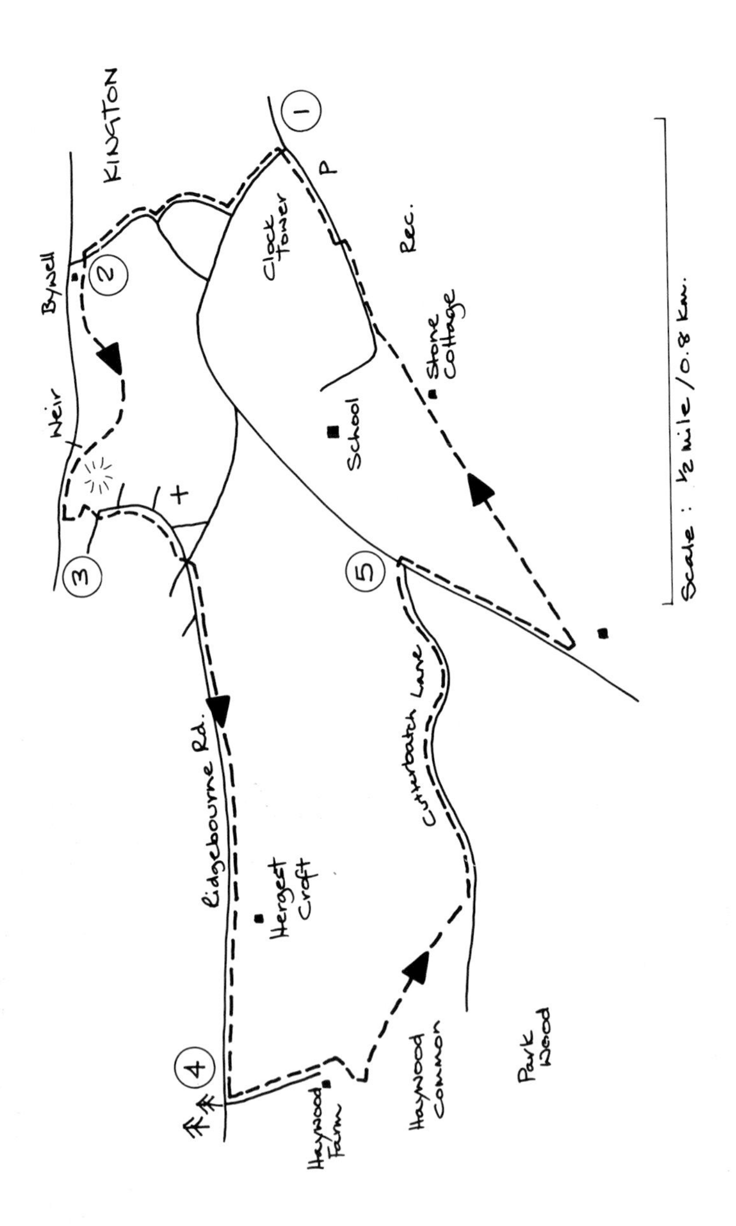
KINGTON
1
P
2
Bywell
Clock Tower
Rec.
Weir
Stone Cottage
School
3
5
Scale : 1/2 mile / 0.8 Km.
Ridgebourne Rd.
Cutterbatch Lane
Hergest Croft
4
Haywood Farm
Haywood Common
Park Wood

LOCAL WALK

Kington **4 miles**

START *From the Town Clock.*

1 *From the Town Clock go up Church St., turn right at the War Memorial, walk through two small squares to the top right corner of the second. Turn right down the hill past the old National School, passing Bradnor View Close on the left.*

2 *Shortly after turn left, by a row of stone cottages, along the old Tram Road. On the right is "Bywell", Wordworth's house with the Scots pine by the gate. Go through a kissing gate and on to the weir on the Back Brook; then another kissing-gate by a cottage, passing a footbridge on your right and on to where the path turns sharply left uphill.*

3 *At the top of the slope turn left on to a lane, bear right at the next fork and then right again at the wall letterbox. Cross the road directly to Ridgebourne Road (signposted "Hergest Croft Gardens") and go up this road for about threequarters of a mile, passing the Gardens on the left.*

4 *Look for a lane on the left by a group of Scots pines on the same side. Turn down here to Haywood Farm, through the yard to an iron gate and on to a downhill track. Follow the line of this with the hedge on the left. The views from here are delightful. At the bottom either divert to "Park Wood" (signposted) to view the rhododendrons, or continue over the cattle grid down Cutterbatch Lane to the Kington-Brilley road.*

5 *Turn right along this road for about 300 yards until you reach Hergest Mill. Take the footpath on the left, turning sharply back towards Kington. Go through three kissing-gates, across the school playing field to the Recreation Ground. Exit by the ornamental gates into Mill Street and on to the Town Clock.*

SHORTWOOD FARM, BETWEEN LEOMINSTER AND BROMYARD

Kington to Lyonshall

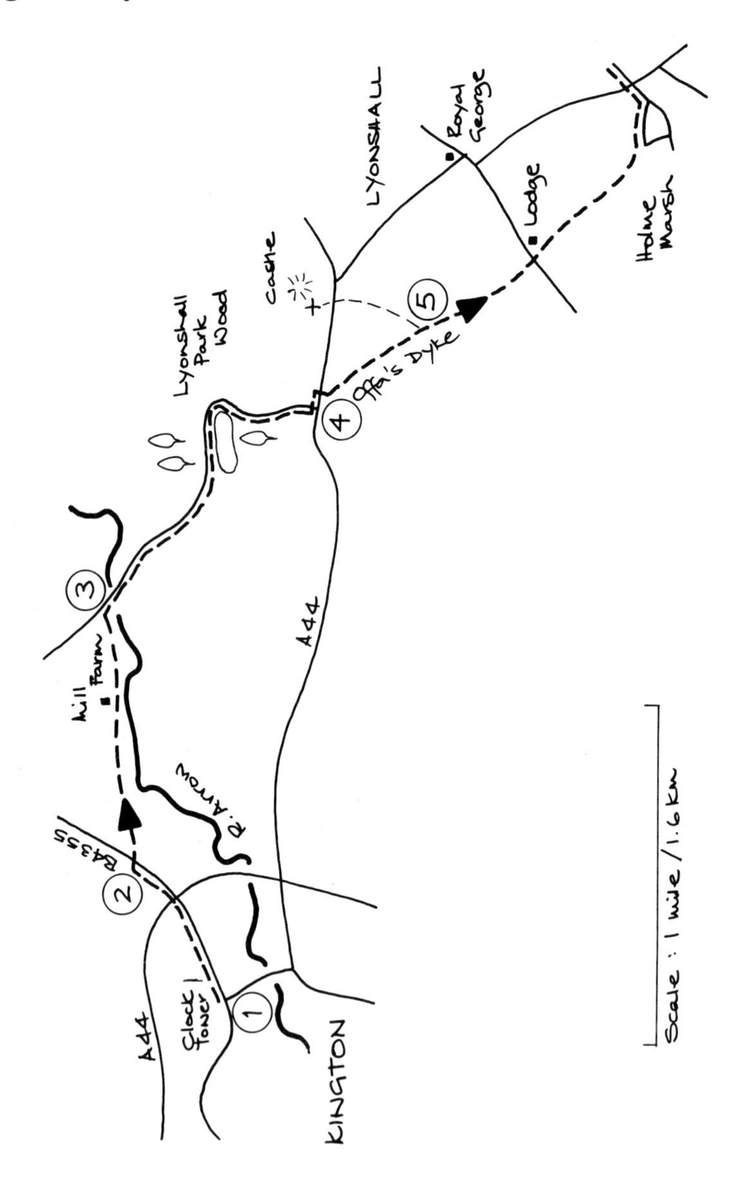

Black and White Trail — Section F

Kington to Lyonshall — 4 miles

START *Kington Clock Tower.*

1 *With your back to the Clock Tower walk along High Street and continue ahead into Victoria Road. This leads to a roundabout where you take the road opposite signed to Titley and Presteigne. Walk facing the traffic and pass an unusual looking house almost hanging over Back Brook before turning right at the next corner along a green lane between two bungalows.*

2 *Go through the gateway and keep ahead to another gate, almost adjacent to the old trackbed of the railway to New Radnor. Keep ahead almost parallel with the old line to cross a stile at the field boundary. Make your way towards Mill Farm, pass through the gate and walk along the track in front of the farmhouse which then sweeps right and left between a wooded bluff and the River Arrow. Go through a gateway into the next pasture and directly ahead to a stile which leads on to a tarmac lane.*

3 *Turn right and follow this lane as it climbs past cottages and woodland for well over half a mile. At the junction beyond Lyonshall Park Wood, go left and at the main A44 road turn left and walk a few paces before crossing with care.*

4 *Cross the stile and turn left. At the corner go right and follow the field's edge for a short distance where the path crosses the field boundary, just beyond where it is joined by the remains of Offa's Dyke and a thick hedge. There's no real stile so many local walkers simply go through the gate on the left beforehand. Walk down the field with the dyke on your right. At the bottom cross the stile on to the track. If visiting the church and castle mound of Lyonshall go left here and retrace steps afterwards.*

5 *Walk a few paces right and then turn left to cross another stile. Head slightly right over the field to cross another stile and then bear left to keep company with the hedge on the left which soon meets a track and gateway, turning immediately right and then left on to the dyke. This short section exits on to a road near to the lodge. If visiting Lyonshall village turn left along the lane for a short distance to the centre. If not, cross the road and walk up the old embankment to the right of the lodge.*

LOCAL WALK

Lyonshall — 1 mile

Outline Lyonshall ~ Old tramway ~ church ~ castle.

Summary A very short pleasant ramble taking in the church and castle ruins.

Attractions There is a puzzle about Lyonshall village. The main part of the settlement is situated at quite a distance from its church and castle. This seems to have been the result of a deliberate move at some time just before the sixteenth century when the Royal George Inn and other houses were built. The castle was still in use in 1473 when an order was given to put the place to rights, but by the beginning of the next century it was once again in disrepair. The only mediaeval house to be found near to the castle is the Wharf at the entrance to Lynhales House, so it looks as if Lyonshall "wandered". This may have been due to a number of factors, although some believe that it was as a result of the Plague that the older village around the castle was abandoned.

The church of St. Michael and All Angels has some relics of its twelfth century origin, but the main part is thirteenth century, restored in 1870 when it was in a ruinous condition. So dangerous was it that as soon as the workmen touched the roof the whole lot fell in with a frightening crash! Today it is in excellent order and is a most attractive, small church.

The Devereux family (see Weobley), under the overlordship of Roger de Lacey, were Lords of the Manor here from around 1090 when the castle was built. The castle ruins, (walls and part of the moat) can be seen just behind the church and constitute the largest amount of standing masonry of any of the castles in the Black and White Trail villages. There was a member of the Devereux family living in the village until quite recently.

The centre of the present village has a group of old houses which includes the Royal George, the old Maidenhead Inn which is now a private residence, the Post Office, Ivy House, Upper House and the Old Forge, outside of which stood the spreading chestnut tree called "Ramsay". The name was given to commemorate the year of its planting as a replacement for the old chestnut which had stood there for centuries. Ramsay referred to Ramsay Macdonald who became Prime Minister in 1930, the year of planting.

When you stand on the smaller road, known as Spond Lane, which joins the main A480 at the Forge and leaves it again alongside the Royal George, your feet are on a highway which has its origin in the Bronze Age, or even earlier times. This same route was used by the Romans as part of their road network linking Mortimer's Cross with Bollingham and on to their fort at Clyro. It is possible that this route was also used by Welsh Saints during the Dark Ages as they brought the light of the Celtic Church to the dark world of the English pagans.

As with Eardisley and Kington the steam railway has come and gone, although railway buffs will notice the bridge abutments in Spond Lane and also on the road down from the church to the Royal George. Just above this latter bridge is the building which was the station on this very typical rural branch line which finally closed in 1940.

Refreshment and Accommodation The Royal George offers a variety of meals as well as good accommodation. Church House also has excellent accommodation and a speciality - afternoon teas, Edwardian Style.

LYONSHALL CHURCH

Lyonshall

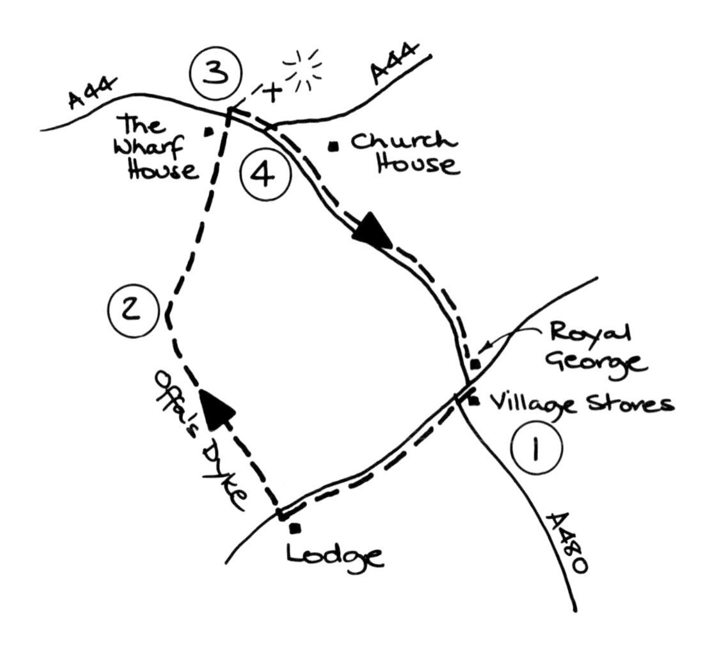

A44
3
A44
The Wharf House
Church House
4
2
Royal George
Village Stores
Offa's Dyke
1
Lodge
A480
Scale: 1 mile /1.6 Km

LOCAL WALK

Lyonshall 1 mile

START *At the Old Forge in Lyonshall village.*

1 *Starting at the Old Forge walk westwards up the Spond Lane. Pass the remnants of a stone railway bridge and a short distance further on turn right through a gateway opposite a lodge cottage. At the next gate, go right and left to follow the hedge to a stile. Cross it and go slightly right to another stile.*

2 *Turn right on the track along the line of the Kington Tramway which in 1820 joined Eardisley to Kington. Continue along the drive to "The Wharf" house at the main road.*

3 *Cross the main road (TAKE CARE!) and take the short lane up to the church. The Castle lies behind the church through a car park.*

4 *On returning to the main road, turn left and go down the hill a short way to where the A480 turn right. Take this road down into the village passing a small iron gateway on the left, next to a lay-by, leading into Church House (see above). Turn right at the Royal George to reach the Forge.*

LYONSHALL (The small tree on the right replaces "The Ramsay")

Lyonshall to Pembridge

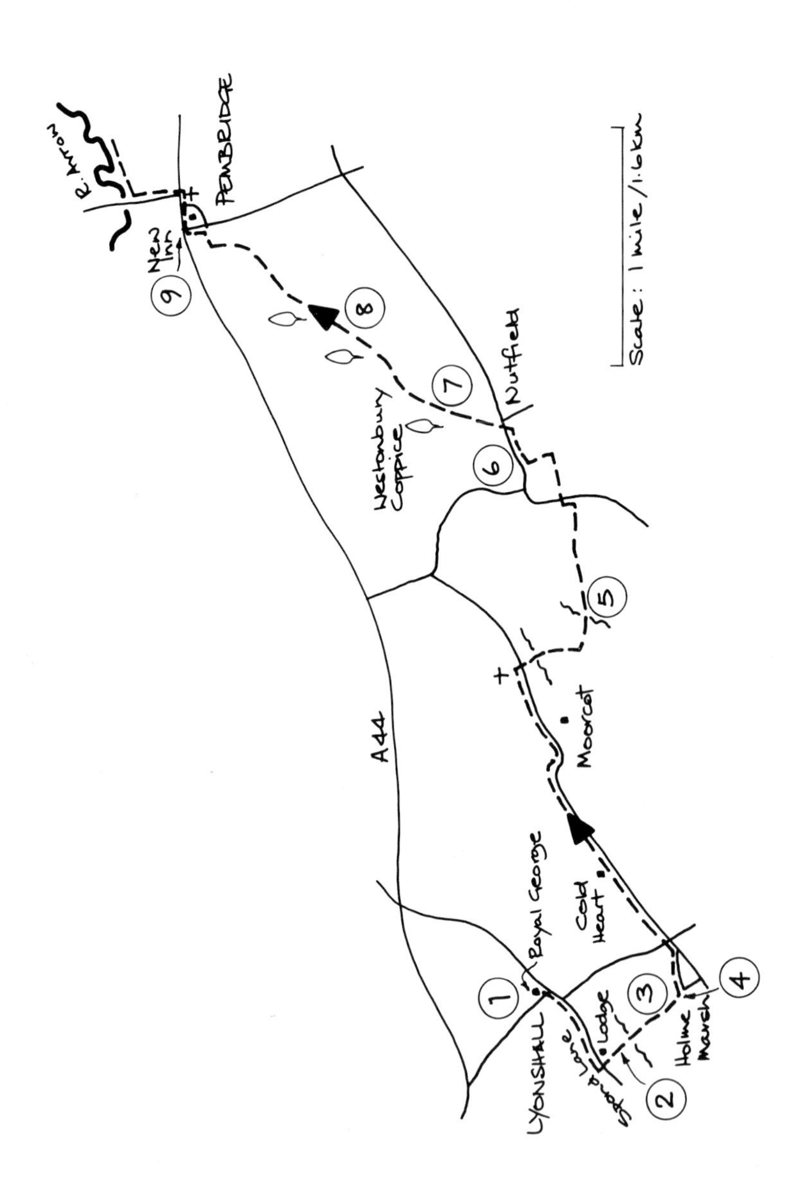

Black and White Trail — Section G

Lyonshall to Pembridge — 9 miles

START *The Royal George Inn, Lyonshall.*

1 *From the Royal George walk on the main A480 towards Hereford and as it bends left, keep ahead along a narrow road, Spond Lane, passing Upper House Farm. Pass the remains of the old railway bridge and a lodge before turning, almost immediately, left up the embankment to the old track bed.*

2 *Look for the path down the other side of the embankment on the left into a field. Keep ahead with the hedge to your right and cross a footbridge.*

3 *Proceed to climb up the hill with the dyke now to your left and cross a track at the top of the field. Go over the stile and head towards the building with an old sunken lane full of rubbish on your right. Look for a stile to the right of the bungalow. Cross this and then proceed along a path which becomes a track.*

4 *At the tarmac lane turn left through the hamlet of Holme Marsh and left at the next junction. Cross the main road and walk down the lane past Cold Heart and Moorcot. Not far beyond is a chapel. At the far end of it look for a stile in the hedge on the right. Cross it and head slightly left to a stile and footbridge. Keep ahead as you walk up the field to join a hedge coming in from the left. In the top left hand corner of the field go left over a stile and then proceed ahead to cross another footbridge.*

5 *Walk to the right of the solitary oak to a stile by a gate and then on to another gateway ahead which leads into a field on the right. Once through, turn left to follow the field edge up to a stile which leads on to a lane. Go left for a few paces and then turn right over a stile and proceed ahead with the hedge to your left. Cross the stile in the corner to a narrower strip. Walk almost to the other side and then turn left. Exit by way of a gate into a lane where you turn right.*

6 *Walk a short distance along the road but when approaching the cottages turn left through a gateway. Proceed towards the next gate ahead but turn right beforehand, to walk along the hedge which is now to your left.*

7 *Go through a wicket gate and walk along the green tracks through Westonbury coppice. Follow the right fork as it curves gently through the wood which soon begins to narrow. The track comes to a barred gate where you leave the wood and keep ahead with the hedge to your left. Go through two gateways as you proceed ahead through large fields to join a track which continues ahead by a coppice. At the T-junction cross the track and pass beneath a large oak into the field.*

8 *Proceed slightly left, passing by three oak trees, to a gateway with wooden rails. Climb over and keep ahead with the hedge to your left. Cross the iron gates in the field corner and walk ahead, once again, with an orchard and farm to the left. You soon come to a gate by an old barn which leads on to a track leading into Pembridge village. Follow the road to the main A44 road where you turn right.*

9 *Turn right again by the New Inn to see the Buttermarket and church. Retrace your steps to the main road which you cross. Just beyond the Red Lion public house turn left and prior to the bridge turn right for the path to Eardisland.*

LOCAL WALK

Pembridge — 2 miles

Outline The Belfry ~ Castle Moat ~ Manley Field ~ Arrow Bridge ~ The Old Steppes.

Summary A walk through orchard and pasture returning to the River Arrow and historic village centre.

Attractions The mediaeval prosperity of this picturesque village produced many buildings of considerable quality which are still to be found in its historic streets. The patronage of the great Mortimer family, whose national influence rose to a peak during the Wars of the Roses in the fifteenth century, ensured its growth. It was during those wars that in 1461 a critical battle took place a few miles away at Mortimer's Cross. Four thousand men died in one day in this ferocious struggle, in which Edward Mortimer, the future Edward IV, defeated the Lancastrian armies and so secured the throne for the House of York.

It is thought that after the battle the treaty was signed in the New Inn, which was only 150 years old at that time! The original inn, the "Old" one, was burned down in 1311 and the present "New Inn" was built soon after.

The sixteenth century Market Hall, which is remarkably like that at Lyons-le-Foret in Normandy, was originally two-storied. It was built on the site of the "mark-stone" (market-stone) which can be seen supporting the timber pillar at the north-east corner of the Hall. Also visible in the pillars are the notches into which the merchants wedged their planks on which they displayed their wares.

When the Market was first granted by Henry III in 1240 this was a trading outpost on the western limits of the kingdom. There was also an Annual May Fair during which the whole village area was filled with buyers and sellers. During the nineteenth century this became a Hiring Fair at which people came to seek employment for the year. This practice ceased in 1920 with the establishment of Employment Exchanges. The May Fair has not taken place since 1946, which is not surprising, as it meant closing the A44 to allow the use of the main street for all the sideshows and stalls.

From the Market Square some steps lead up to the church and alongside it the magnificent timber belfry for which Pembridge is famous. This three-storey structure of stone and timber, built in the fourteenth century, is very reminiscent of the timber stave churches in Norway. It houses the bells and a clock mechanism, all of which can be viewed from inside. The church is also fourteenth century and its size is another indication of the prosperity of this settlement at that time.

As well as the New Inn there is the Pembridge Inn, built in the sixteenth century. This is a fine example of close-set timbering being used to display prosperity as well as to support the building. As one might expect for such old hostelries there are ghost stories attached to both. In the coaching days of th eighteenth and early nineteenth century the London to Aberystwyth mail came through Pembridge, and the New Inn became known to travellers as "The Inn without a Name".

A fine building which is often overlooked is the great barn at Court House, just up the road from the Market Place towards Luntley. This barn still has the central arch through which the haywains passed for unloading, as well as many other features indicating a sizeable farming enterprise. Through the arch are other fine timber framed farm buildings, although the third range beyond has been pulled down.

Court House itself is a wonderful mixture of periods and styles, which, as it has been a homestead for so long, is not surprising. It was the home of one of the original Herefordshire Cattle Herds.

A walk through the village will reveal many fine timber-framed buildings. The Olde Steppes shop, beside the entrance to the churchyard was the Rectory until 1777. Other houses indicate their past purpose by their names:- the Forge, the Wheelwrights, the Almshouses. The two rows of almshouses, Duppa's and Trafford's on the Leominster road were built in the seventeenth century and it is worth walking along the main street to look at the inscription left by the builder on Trafford's Almshouses!

For a cool, quiet break from the A44 there is the land beside the three-arched bridge over the River Arrow which can be reached by going down Bridge Street (opposite the Olde Steppes). This is not so attractive in the winter after heavy rain as the Arrow is likely to flood the low-lying land there.

Another diversion when in Pembridge is to take the Luntley road from the Market Place, following the signs to Dunkerton's Cider. Here it is possible to see and taste Herefordshire cider made in the traditional way with specific types of cider apples.

Accommodation and Refreshment These are available from the Pembridge, New and Red Lion inns. There are also a number of homes offering Bed and Breakfast, both in the village and just outside it. Some of these belong to the Country Village Weekends group and bookings can be made through the village representative (see Appendix).

There is a Post Office in the Market Place.

There is a limited bus service to Hereford, Kington and Leominster.

Pembridge

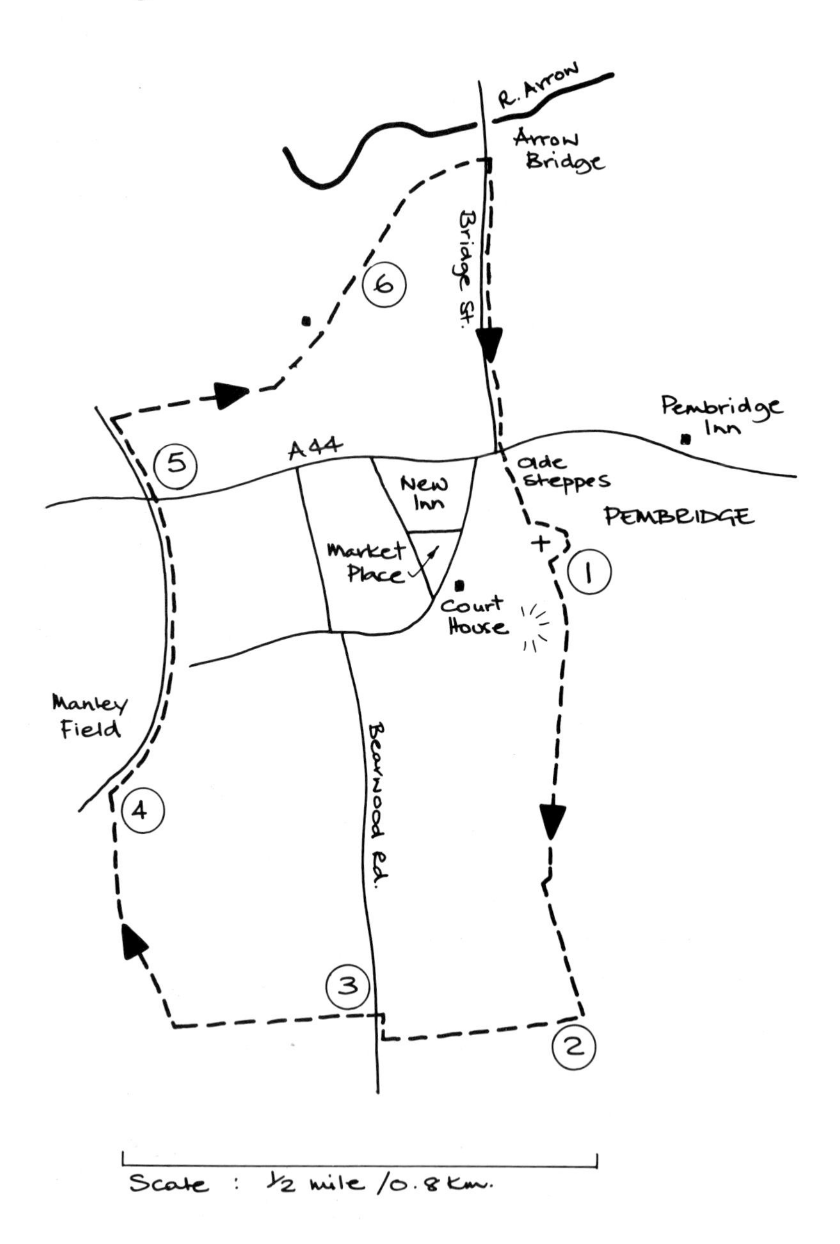
R. Arrow
Arrow Bridge
Bridge St.
6
Pembridge Inn
A44
5
Olde Steppes
New Inn
PEMBRIDGE
Market Place
1
Court House
Manley Field
Bearwood Rd.
4
3
2
Scale : ½ mile / 0.8 km.

LOCAL WALK

Pembridge **2 miles**

START *At Pembridge church.*

1 *Take the path round the east end of the church to a kissing-gate. Follow the right-hand hedge to the corner by the old Moat. Cross into a large field, heading for the far right corner. Cross into the fruit farm field and take the track along the left-hand hedge until it is joined by another track on the right which separates fruit bushes from trees.*

2 *Turn right along this track to a stile in the hedge. Cross the stile on to Bearwood Road. Turn right and walk for twenty yards. Turn left through a gate into a field.*

3 *Keeping close to the hedge on the right, cross the field to the right-hand corner and take a stile to the right. Keep to the left-hand hedge, through an iron gate, another field and another iron gate into a green lane.*

4 *Turn right into the lane and continue until houses are reached and then the A44. Cross the road to an entrance gate between cottages which leads to another green lane.*

5 *Go down the lane to reach a stile on the right. Cross this, then keeping a hedge on the right cross the field, through a gate, into a second field. Bear diagonally left across the field, keeping a telegraph pole to the left, and aiming for the corner of backgardens to houses ahead.*

6 *Cross a stile into a steep, sometimes muddy, field above the River Arrow. Walk diagonally across the slope towards the end of the garden nearest the river. Go along the side of the garden/drive to a stile next to Arrow Bridge. Cross the stile and turn right into Bridge Street, leading to the A44 and the Olde Steppes. Climb the steps beside the shop to return to the churchyard and the Belfry.*

THE NEW INN, PEMBRIDGE (14th Century)

Pembridge to Eardisland

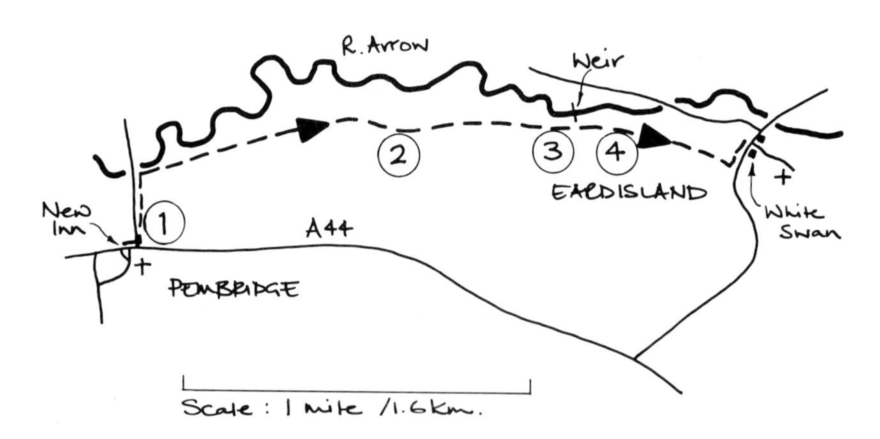

PEMBRIDGE BELFRY

Black and White Trail — Section H

Pembridge to Eardisland — 3 miles

START *New Inn, Pembridge.*

1 *From the New Inn return to and cross the main A44 road. Turn left just beyond the Red Lion public house into the Shobdon road. Before the bridge over the River Arrow turn right and pass delightful riverside seats to cross a stile into a long flat flood plain. Keep ahead, close to the hedge on the right, rather than being tempted to walk along the riverside for the right of way is not clear to follow.*

2 *Cross a bridge guarded by stiles in the next field boundary, a little to the right of a mid hedge point. Enter the next field. Go slightly left in this next field of equally large dimensions towards the field corner opposite using two isolated oaks as a directional guide. At the corner keep ahead, with drainage ditch and hedge now to your right and cross a stile.*

3 *Proceed ahead through a small field to another stile by a weir on the Arrow. Cross the stile and follow the green path around the left of the field which leads to a narrow and nettled track, but fortunately you go right to cross two stiles between hazel and elder.*

4 *Turn left and follow the field edge and waymark arrow to another double stile, now with views of Eardisland village and church. A finger post on a second stile reads "Eardisland" and points ahead, to the left of a truncated hawthorn hedge and on to a stile by the houses. Go left to pass by the Swan and Cross inns.*

17th CENTURY ALMSHOUSES, PEMBRIDGE

LOCAL WALK

Eardisland **3 miles**

Outline Eardisland ~ Sytches Coppice ~ Burton Court ~ Eardisland.

Summary A romantic short ramble with numerous kissing-gates, across fields to Burton Court returning by way of a lane and paths into the village. Passes by Eardisland church.

Attractions For many people Eardisland is the dream image of an English village, with its half-timbered cottages on the grassy banks of a clear stream slipping quietly under the old stone bridge. Who could not be happy in such a place? Strange to relate, someone once had to be paid to be happy there! Admittedly it was over 900 years ago when the sizeable, and prosperous settlement belonged to the Earl Morcar of Northumbria. The Domesday Book records that in previous years the Reeve of Eardisland gave Earl Morcar's Lady 18 ounces of pence (about 290 pence) annually "so that she might be happy".

The bridge is a natural point from which to see some of the most interesting buildings, with the Old School House (and its whipping post!) alongside, and the Manor House and its dovecot opposite. A short distance on the left along the Leominster road is the fine Staick House dating from around 1300. This was a Yeoman's Hall at first and then later became the Mote House or Council Chamber where legal matters were dealt with. The house was added to from the fourteenth to the fifteenth centuries and there are traces of these additions apparent to the external observer today.

The bridge has been rebuilt on a number of occasions but the eighteenth century version lasted until the Second World War when a U.S. Army artillery convoy damaged it considerably. It was rebuilt with a wider carriageway but using the eighteenth century stonework as a facing.

The parish church of St. Mary the Virgin dates from 1200 with additions in the fourteenth and fifteenth centuries. The timber roof dates from this time and is an interesting example of mediaeval roof structures.

Another very fine roof is to be found in the Great Hall of Burton Court, which lies about a mile outside the village. This site, of strategic importance from pre-Roman times, was where Henry, Prince of Wales, later to become King Henry V, set up his headquarters in the campaign against the Welsh nationalist, Owain Glyndwr, in 1402. The Great Hall would have been known to him, although the outside of the building today would not, as it consists of additions over the years, principally in Regency times. The present entrance was designed in 1912 by Sir Clough William-Ellis, of Portmeirion fame, to replace a Gothic-style doorway. The house is usually open to the public in the afternoons from the Spring Bank Holiday to mid-September.

Refreshment and Accommodation The Cross Inn and the White Swan offer meals and snacks. A Traditional Tea-rooms, gift shop and garden opposite the church provides light meals throughout the day, and can offer general tourist advice.

THE RIVER ARROW AT EARDISLAND

Eardisland

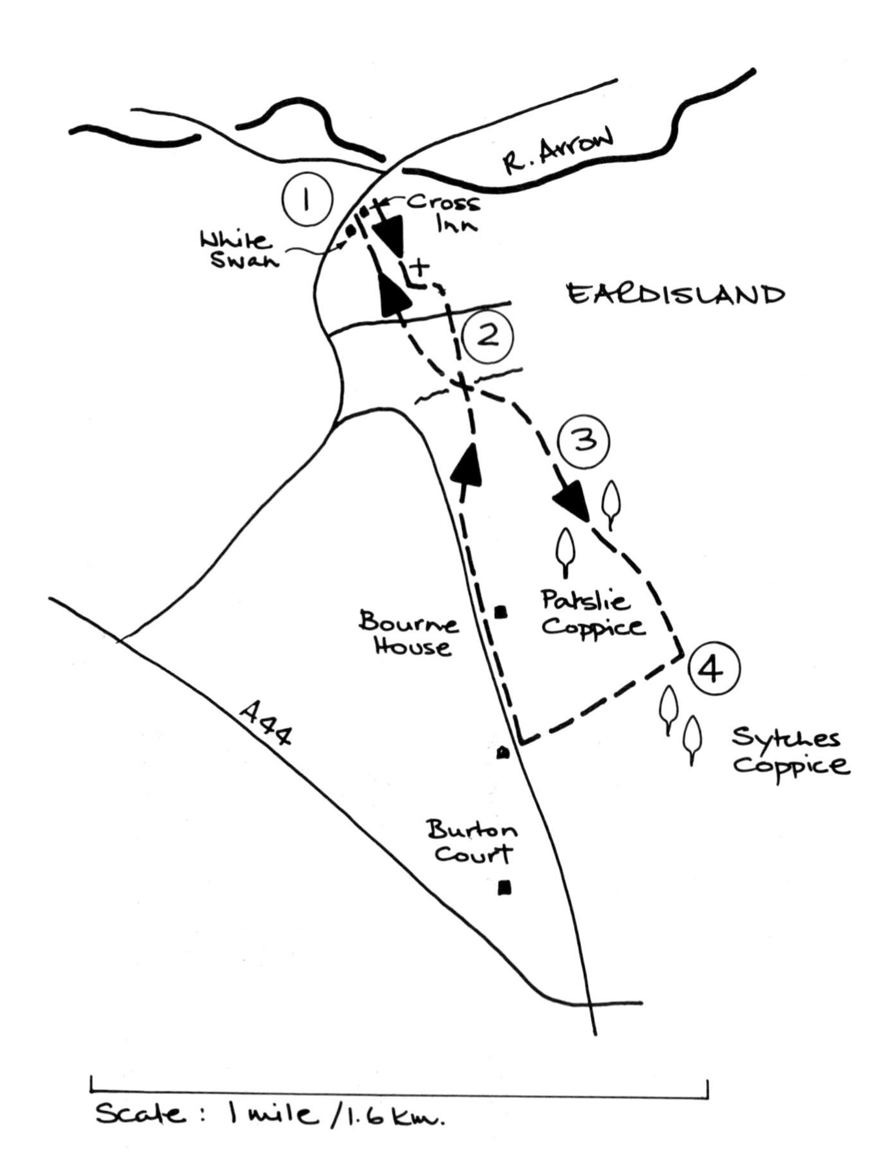

R. Arrow
1
Cross Inn
White Swan
EARDISLAND
2
3
4
Parslie Coppice
Bourne House
Sytches Coppice
A44
Burton Court
Scale: 1 mile / 1.6 km.

LOCAL WALK

Eardisland **3 miles**

START *From the Cross Inn.*

1 *From the inn turn right and pass through the gate by the farm on your right before the bridge. Walk through the muddy farmyard to a kissing-gate and another small gate which brings you to Eardisland church. Pass to the left of the church and keep ahead through the churchyard to a small gap where you turn right along a short length of path to a tarmac lane.*

2 *Keep ahead to pass by an old school and then to cross another gate. Go through the narrow pasture to another kissing-gate and over a stream, then turn left to cross a stile. Head across the field to the right of a very large oak and cross another stile.*

3 *There is no clear landmark in the next field. Keep ahead towards the wood, Patslie Coppice, until you reach the stile and bridge over the ditch. Walk slightly left through the woodland to another stile. Once over go left along the field boundary and go through a barred gate. Climb up the field's edge, through a gateway and up to another gate by Sytches Coppice.*

4 *Go through the gate and turn right to follow the hedge to a stile by a gate which leads on to a tarmac road. Bear left if continuing to Burton Court which appears shortly on the right. If not, turn right and walk down the road and after passing Bourne House look for a kissing-gate on the right and go through it. In the field bear slightly left to cross the brook once again but then go left through the playing field to a track by a cottage. This leads to a tarmac lane. Go left and immediately right to pass by the church, tearoom and to the inns on the main road.*

DILWYN VILLAGE GREEN

Eardisland to Leominster

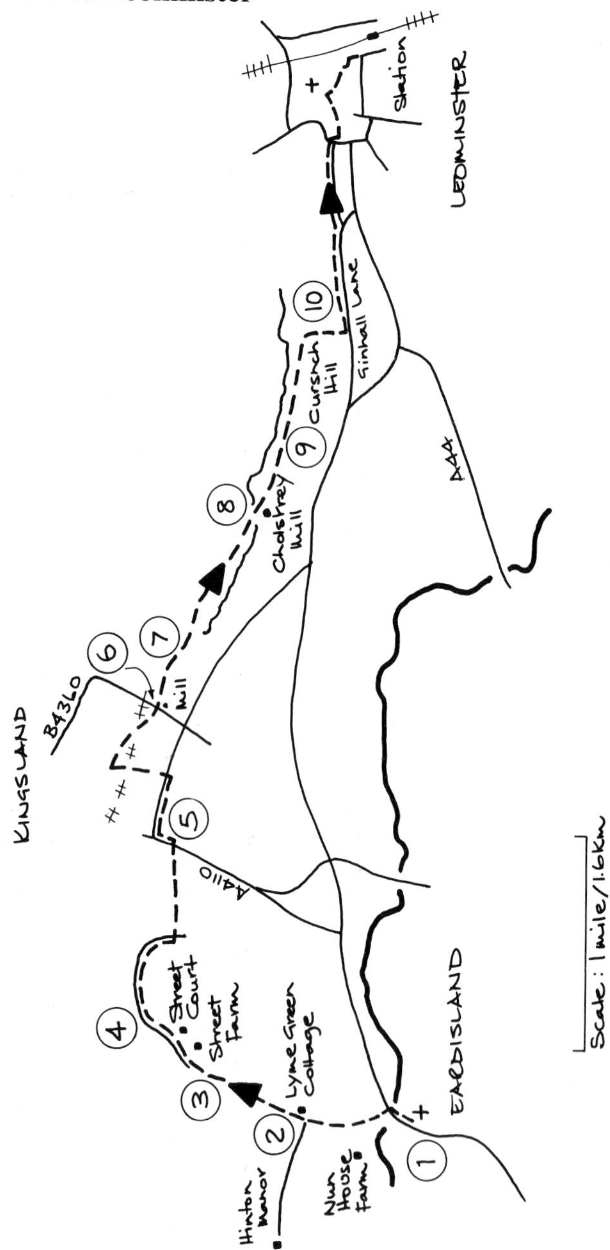

Black and White Trail — Section I

Eardisland to Leominster — 11 miles

START *The Swan Inn, Eardisland.*

1 *From the entrance of the Swan Inn turn right, cross the bridge and turn second left along a narrow lane by a magnificent example of a timber framed house. The road has a 'No Through Road' sign. Follow this lane, avoiding a right turn at first and then a left turn to Nun House Farm. Not far beyond, as the road curves to the entrance of Hinton Manor Farm turn right to pass by Lyme Green Cottage.*

2 *Go through iron gates into a field and keep ahead to another gate. Once through, head slightly left to another gateway just to the left of the oak trees. Go through and proceed slightly right to another gate. Then head up the next field with the hedge on the left to go through a barred gate into an orchard.*

3 *Go through another gateway and then head slightly right towards a track leading to farm buildings. Once on the track pass Street Farm on the right and follow the tarmac road to the left of Street Court. At the next junction turn right.*

4 *Follow the lane as it curves gently right. The road begins to climb and you see a bungalow ahead. Look for a green track cutting off left which leads to the main A4110 road.*

5 *Cross the road with caution and turn left. At the junction go right and walk facing the traffic for a quarter of a mile, passing the industrial estate and then Venn Bridge House. Just beyond cross the road and go left into the field as signed. Walk ahead with the hedge to your right, cross the old railway track bed and proceed ahead once again towards the church. Cross two footbridges in succession and then turn right (unless visiting Kingsland village -keep ahead for a short distance to pass by the church).*

6 *Follow the hedge and stream on the right to cross a stile. Keep ahead again to cross another two stiles and enter an orchard. Exit by way of the gate into the B4360 road by the old railway. Turn right for a few steps and then cross the road and stile by the mill. Walk by the old mill stream along the field to a gateway with the sewage works now to your left.*

7 *Pass through another gateway and go right across the field to the far right corner. Cross the stile and keep ahead near to the meanders of the Pinsley Brook eventually coming to another stile and with Cholstrey Mill now in view. As the stream bends right go ahead to cross another stile and walk ahead just to the right of the oak trees. Cross the stile by the gate and keep ahead again with the fence and hedge to your right.*

8 *Approach the mill by going right through the barred gate and ahead to the mill house. The right of way is ahead by the old mill building but as this is difficult ramblers usually pass to the left of the house then turn right to exit by a gateway as the lane climbs and curves right. You, however, go left as signed along a concrete track and as it begins to curve left keep ahead to cross another stile and to follow the banks of the brook.*

continued on page 64

9 *Cross the next stile into a field where Cursneh Hill rises but the path curves left to a stile by a gate and follows a green track at the foot of the hill to exit by way of a stile on to a track by a cottage. Go right and follow the track to Ginhall Lane.*

10 *Turn left into the lane and walk gently uphill for approximately one quarter of a mile. Turn left into Green Lane, with a view now of Leominster Priory, and at the main road turn right and cross into Rainbow Street. Turn left into Burgess Street and cross into Church Street which leads to the priory. Leave by way of the other side of the play area on the right into Pinsley Road. This twists right and left at least once before joining Etnam Street for the short return section ahead to the railway station.*
